THE MICHELIN GUIDE

WASHINGTON DC

MICHELIN

THE MICHELIN GUIDE'S COMMITMENTS

Whether they are in Japan, the USA, China or Europe, our inspectors apply the same criteria to judge the quality of each and every establishment that they visit. The MICHELIN guide commands a **worldwide reputation** thanks to the commitments we make to our readers—and we reiterate these below:

Our inspectors make **anonymous visits** to restaurants to gauge the quality of cuisine offered to the everyday customer. They pay their own bill and make no indication of their presence. These visits are supplemented by comprehensive monitoring of information—our readers' comments are one valuable source, and are always taken into consideration.

Our choice of establishments is a completely **independent** one, made for the benefit of our readers alone. Decisions are discussed by the inspectors and editor, with the most important considered at the global level. Inclusion in the Guide is always free of charge.

The Guide offers a **selection** of the best restaurants in each category of comfort and price. A recommendation in the Guide is an honor in itself, and defines the establishment among the "best of the best."

All practical information, the classifications, and awards are revised and updated every year to ensure the most **reliable information** possible.

The standards and criteria for the classifications are the same in all countries covered by the MICHELIN guides. Our system is used worldwide and easy to apply when selecting a restaurant.

As part of Michelin's ongoing commitment to improving **travel and mobility**, we do everything possible to make vacations and eating out a pleasure.

THE MICHELIN GUIDE'S SYMBOLS

Michelin inspectors are experts at finding the best restaurants and invite you to explore the diversity of the gastronomic universe. As well as evaluating a restaurant's cooking, we also consider its décor, the service and the ambience – in other words, the all-round culinary experience.

Two keywords help you make your choice more quickly: red for the type of cuisine, gold for the atmosphere.

Italian • Elegant

FACILITIES & SERVICES

🍇	Notable wine list
🍹	Notable cocktail list
🍺	Notable beer list
🍶	Notable sake list
♿	Wheelchair accessible
⛱	Outdoor dining
🍳	Breakfast
🥐	Brunch
🥢	Dim sum
⊟	Private dining room
💵	Cash only

AVERAGE PRICES

👄	Under $25
$$	$25 to $50
$$$	$50 to $75
$$$$	Over $75

STARS

Our famous one ❀, two ❀❀ and three ❀❀❀ stars identify establishments serving the highest quality cuisine – taking into account the quality of ingredients, the mastery of techniques and flavors, the levels of creativity and, of course, consistency.

❀❀❀	Exceptional cuisine, worth a special journey
❀❀	Excellent cuisine, worth a detour
❀	High quality cooking, worth a stop

BIB GOURMAND

Inspectors' favorites for good value.

MICHELIN PLATE

Good cooking.
Fresh ingredients, capably
prepared: simply a good meal.

DEAR READER,

It's been an exciting year for the entire team at the MICHELIN guides in North America, and it is with great pride that we present you with our 2019 edition to Washington DC. Over the past year, our inspectors have extended their reach to include a variety of establishments and multiplied their anonymous visits to restaurants in our selection in order to accurately reflect the rich culinary diversity this great city has to offer.

As part of the Guide's highly confidential and meticulous evaluation process, our inspectors have methodically eaten their way through the entire city with a mission to marshal the finest in each category for your enjoyment. While they are expertly trained professionals in the food industry, the Guides remain consumer-driven and provide comprehensive choices to accommodate your every comfort, taste and budget. By dining and drinking as "everyday" customers, they are able to experience and evaluate the same level of service and cuisine as any other guest. This past year has seen some unique advancements in DC's dining scene.

Our company's founders, Édouard and André Michelin, published the first MICHELIN guide in 1900, to provide motorists with useful information about where they could service and repair their cars as well as find a good quality meal. In 1926, the star-rating system was introduced, whereby outstanding establishments are awarded for excellence in cuisine. Over the decades we have made many new enhancements to the Guide, and the local team here in Washington DC eagerly carries on these traditions.

As we take consumer feedback seriously, please feel free to contact us at: michelin.guides@michelin.com. You may also follow our Inspectors on Instagram (@michelininspectors) as they eat their way around town. We thank you for your patronage and truly hope that the MICHELIN guide will remain your preferred reference to Washington DC's restaurants.

CONTENTS

■ RESTAURANTS 10

■ MAPS 86

■ INDEXES

WASHINGTON DC

A RAKE'S PROGRESS ▮◯

American • *Trendy*

MAP: 2-A3

Drama? Yes, please. A Rake's Progress is no ordinary dining room, and the Line is not your workaday hotel. Housed inside a gorgeous old stone church in Adams Morgan, this "rakish" room shoots big and scores. The dining area offers a sweeping vision of the gorgeous lobby from its second floor perch; while nearby, an open fire hearth illuminates the bustling open kitchen.

The menu is a celebration of American agriculture, built on ingredients specifically found in the Mid-Atlantic region. The offerings rotate with the season, and meat-free courses make a bold statement. A vegetable mille-feuille is tucked with roasted, grilled and smoked root vegetables before being softly piled over aerated cream studded with charred ramps and cheddar croutons.

▮ 1770 Euclid St. NW (at Champlain St.)

☎ (202) 588-0525 — **WEB:** www.thelinehotel.com/dc

▮ Dinner nightly   PRICE: $$$

AL TIRAMISU ▮◯

Italian • *Osteria*

MAP: 1-B2

With two decades under its belt, it's clear that Al Tiramisu is no flash in the pan. The unassuming restaurant is classic Italian down to the paintings of the Old Country and shelves lined with homemade limoncello. And, for the crowd of diplomats and intellectuals who flock here, these anything-but-trendy environs are precisely the draw.

Though the food is rustic at its core, presentation is nothing if not elegant; and Chef Luigi Diotaiuti's dedication to ingredients has been recognized by DC Slow Food. Menu highlights include toothsome pappardelle tossed with sliced portobello mushrooms in a deliciously savory sauce, as well as grilled fish, lamb chops and roast chicken. Whatever you choose, be sure to save room for the namesake—and just right—tiramisu.

▮ 2014 P St. NW (bet. Hopkins & 20th Sts.)

▮ Dupont Circle

☎ (202) 467-4466 — **WEB:** www.altiramisu.com

▮ Lunch Mon – Fri Dinner nightly   PRICE: $$

ALL PURPOSE 🍴

Italian • *Pizzeria*

MAP: 3-A1

Everyone's buzzing about this Shaw neighborhood gem, courtesy of The Red Hen's gifted chef, Mike Friedman, and his talented partners. Don't be surprised to find a queue if you can't snag a reservation, but dinner is well worth the wait. Inside, discover a cozy space featuring mosaic-tile floors, distressed walls and an open kitchen. A second location has cropped up at the Capitol Riverfront.

This menu offers a handful of perfectly light pizzas topped with a creative mix of fresh ingredients. Italian plates round out the offerings—imagine plump globes of burrata paired with chickpea pancakes; crispy garlic knots; and Jersey-style eggplant parm. Don't miss the gorgeous desserts, turned out by the artistic Tiffany MacIsaac (of Buttercream Bakeshop).

▨ 1250 9th St. NW (bet. M & N Sts.)
🚇 Shaw-Howard U
📞 (202) 849-6174 — **WEB:** www.allpurposedc.com
▨ Lunch Mon – Sat Dinner nightly   PRICE: $$

AMBAR 👻

Balkan • *Rustic*

MAP: 4-C2

Don't balk at trying something new, since Ambar rewards rookies with a lineup of enticing offerings at appealing prices. This two-story restaurant's rustic-country décor is as well suited to groups as it is to solo diners.

Come with a gang and eat to your heart's content with the Balkan Experience, which is a litany of delightful small plates. Don't fret if you're sans friends though, as everyone is guaranteed a good time. Order the chef's platter and you'll be treated to the likes of pita sa sirom, a flaky cheese pie resting in a red bell pepper- and eggplant-ajvar sauce. Partake in the veal and beef kebabs set in a sheep's milk cheese spread; or sour cabbage stuffed with rice, pork belly and set atop garlicky mashed potatoes for even more fun.

▨ 523 8th St. SE (bet. E & G Sts.)
🚇 Eastern Market
📞 (202) 813-3039 — **WEB:** www.ambarrestaurant.com
▨ Lunch & dinner daily   PRICE: $$

ANA

Contemporary · Wine bar

MAP: 4-A4

Set along the Navy Yard's breezy riverfront, this sister spot to New York City's Brooklyn Winery opened in fall of 2017. Though its wine list features bottles from a host of American regions, it notably has the honor of serving wines produced from DC's first winery, located on premises and headed up by winemaker, Conor McCormack.

Inside the upscale-industrial space, you'll find a glass wall offering views of the winemaking facilities, a tasting area and dining room with floor-to-ceiling windows overlooking the Anacostia River. The menu dishes up global inspiration in colorful plates like the golden beet muhammara; kampachi crudo with rhubarb ponzu; grilled octopus with pineapple aguachile; and spring vegetable pithivier with black truffle vinaigrette.

- 385 Water St. SE (at 4th St.)
- Navy Yard-Ballpark
- (202) 484-9210 — **WEB:** www.districtwinery.com
- Lunch & dinner daily   PRICE: $$

ANXO

Basque · Tapas bar

MAP: 2-D4

This cider house rules. Anxo focuses on cider and small plates hailing from the Basque region. Downstairs, the pintxos bar and wood casks lend a fun, traditional flair, while upstairs has a raw, industrial-meets-rustic appearance. And speaking of which, pintxos (an offering of bite-sized tapas) may include marinated mussels, bacalao fritters, oyster mushroom-stuffed piquillos, chistorra sausage and aged Manchego among others. The local heirloom red and yellow tomato salad with shaved onion and balsamic vinegar is simply delicious. Stuffed txipiron (squid) is set over caramelized onions, while the Onaga red snapper escabeche, grilled à la plancha, rests in a deliciously tart marinade.

Not into cider? Basque wines, sherries and vermouths do the trick.

- 300 Florida Ave. NW (at 3rd St.)
- Shaw-Howard U
- (202) 986-3795 — **WEB:** www.anxodc.com
- Lunch Sat – Sun Dinner nightly   PRICE: $$

BAD SAINT 😊
Filipino · *Cozy*

MAP: 2-C2

You'll need the patience of a saint to dine here as they don't take reservations and have no phone to prove the point; but good things do come to those who wait. Once inside, the mood is appealingly boisterous; and seats are in the thick of it all—near the kitchen. The chef isn't letting his fame go to his head and he's still upping his game, creating many Filipino adobos and other flavor-packed dynamo dishes.

Sisig arrives on a sizzling plate with chopped pork jowl and a raw egg cracked in the center for hot and creamy goodness. Then dig into kinilaw na pugita, a ceviche-style dish, followed by deep-fried apples nestled inside spring roll wrappers. There's only one dessert option on the oft-changing menu, but chances are that it will be a great treat.

▦ 3226 11th St. NW (bet. Kenyon & Lamont Sts.)
🚇 Columbia Heights
✆ N/A — **WEB:** www.badsaintdc.com
▦ Dinner Wed – Mon   PRICE: $$

BIDWELL 😊
American · *Contemporary décor*

 ♿

MAP: 8-A2

You will indeed fare well at Bidwell, tucked inside Union Market with its array of stalls peddling everything from arepas to empanadas. This place checks off all of the boxes for a modern hot spot with its industrial-chic design, hipster-packed bar and buzz-worthy food. Bidwell takes the farm-to-table trend and tops it—quite literally— since the rooftop garden supplies much of the kitchen's produce.

The menu has so much to offer with the likes of lobster tacos, daily sausage specials and wood-fired pizzas with four different crust styles (charcoal-activated, anyone?). Intriguing toppings make these pizzas the jam; try the clam pie marrying meaty mollusks with rooftop kale, Benton's bacon, béchamel sauce and mozzarella for lip-smacking results.

▦ 1309 5th St. NE (in Union Market)
🚇 NoMa-Gallaudet U
✆ (202) 547-0172 — **WEB:** www.bidwelldc.com
▦ Lunch & dinner Tue – Sun   PRICE: $$

THE BIRD

Contemporary · *Neighborhood*

MAP: 3-A1

Most everyone loves chicken, but The Bird turns something that seems like a safe bet into a very worthy dinner. Meals commence with a wink to the menu's celebration of poultry by offering diners a complimentary bowl of "bird seed"—a savory mix of pepitas, sunflower seeds and raisins. The humble chicken reaches for new heights here, finding global influence in the crunchy, sweet and spicy Korean wings sprinkled with cilantro; grilled chicken draped in bright red peri-peri sauce; or duck meatballs in tomato curry. Count on the brunch menu to highlight myriad egg creations.

Located near Logan Circle, the bi-level space is lively and festooned with custom works from local artists. If pork is more your style though, try sibling restaurant, The Pig.

■ 1337 11th St. NW (at O St.)
🚇 Mt Vernon Sq
📞 (202) 518-3609 — **WEB:** www.thebirddc.com
■ Lunch Sat – Sun Dinner nightly   **PRICE:** $$

BLACKSALT

Seafood · *Neighborhood*

MAP: 7-B1

Fried, wood-grilled, simmered, steamed or raw. No, it's not a line from Forrest Gump. As long as it swims, you can have it any way you want it at BlackSalt. It's all fish, all the time at this market-cum-restaurant in Palisades. There is a lively, bistro vibe here, where the bar is made for a cocktail and a platter of freshly shucked oysters; while private booths appeal to a sophisticated, mature crowd.

The concise menu trawls coast to continent for inspiration, with dishes such as fried Ipswich clams and fish tacos to Provençal stew. Bigeye tuna tartare is silky; and potato-crusted skate wing is topped with a fragrant brown butter-mustard vinaigrette.

Hit the market on the way out for gourmet items to stock the pantry and soups to fill the freezer.

■ 4883 MacArthur Blvd. (bet. U & V Sts.)
📞 (202) 342-9101 — **WEB:** www.blacksaltrestaurant.com
■ Lunch & dinner daily   **PRICE:** $$

Proud sponsor of the 2019 Washington, D.C. Michelin Guide.

UNITED AIRLINES

Cuisine and travel have always gone hand-in-hand, and a superior experience in either one is worth celebrating.

That's why we're excited to team up with the *Michelin Guide North America* as their Official Airline sponsor, serving Chicago, New York, San Francisco and Washington, D.C.

fly the friendly skies

BLUE DUCK TAVERN ✿

American • *Contemporary décor*

MAP: 1-A2

Simply put, Blue Duck Tavern will have you at hello. Set within the Park Hyatt hotel, this upscale American tavern boasts a sleek, urbane and dreamily sprawling interior, with its 25-foot entry doors, floor-to-ceiling windows, walnut wood seating and highly coveted glass-enclosed booths. (And if that doesn't have you swooning, the dessert station, piled high with tempting treats, certainly will.) Whether seated in the plush dining room or expansive lounge—which features a totally separate cheese- and charcuterie-focused menu— the gorgeous space and its well-to-do crowd are the epitome of casual sophistication.

Much like the space, the product-driven menu has an all-American sensibility. At the center of the massive open kitchen sits a wood-burning oven, a behemoth centerpiece that turns out everything from whole fish and tea-smoked duck breast to the signature roasted bone marrow. Expect some big dishes like foie gras crème brûlée or braised beef rib and Brussels sprouts in a Bourbon-ginger glaze. Portions are generous; split the oven-roasted veal rack to avoid being overstuffed.

Staying at the hotel? You are a lucky duck indeed, as room service is handled by the restaurant.

■ 1201 24th St. NW (bet. M & N Sts.)
🚇 Foggy Bottom-GWU
✆ (202) 419-6755 – **WEB:** www.blueducktavern.com
■ Lunch & dinner daily   PRICE: $$$

BOMBAY CLUB
Indian • Elegant

MAP: 1-C4

A fixture on the DC scene for a number of decades now, this Penn Quarter stalwart, owned by the affable Ashok Bajaj, still functions as a club for politicians and Beltway insiders. Polished and sophisticated with just a hint of spice, Bombay Club's environs are a nostalgic nod to the British clubs of the Raj.

If you can take your eyes off the senator snuggled into the half-moon banquette, the polished Indian cuisine doesn't disappoint. Palate-pleasing items span the continent to include Northern grilled meats, as well as Southern seafood and coconut-inflected dishes. Tender minced lamb is coaxed with a hint of heat in the Seekh kebab, while the bharli vangi's soft-as-pudding bulbs of stuffed and braised baby eggplant simply burst with flavor.

- 815 Connecticut Ave. NW (bet. H & I Sts.)
- Farragut West
- (202) 659-3727 — **WEB:** www.bombayclubdc.com
- Lunch Sun – Fri Dinner nightly   **PRICE:** $$$

BOQUERIA
Spanish • Tapas bar

MAP: 1-B2

Boqueria may be an import from New York City, but the flavor is straight up Spain. This slightly creaky row home belies the stylish and modern interior. Head upstairs for a tête-à-tête, while the main level's bar displaying meats and cheeses whets the appetite for what's to come. And what is to come? Tapas, tapas and more tapas. Sure, there are salads and sandwiches, but with all-day small plates tempting you, why diverge?

The offerings are familiar, with plenty of Spanish classics (croquetas, those fried fritters of gooey deliciousness, for one), but contemporary creations make their mark. Colorado lamb meatballs in a rich tomato sauce with sheep's milk cheese are spot on, while pulpo a la plancha over olive oil-mashed potatoes delivers a pop of flavor.

- 1837 M St. NW (at 19th St.)
- Farragut North
- (202) 558-9545 — **WEB:** www.boqueriadc.com
- Lunch & dinner daily   **PRICE:** $$

BRESCA

Contemporary • *Trendy*

MAP: 2-B4

It may be located on bustling 14th Street, but beautiful Bresca far from blends in with the crowd. Instead, this inviting restaurant mixes the warmth of a neighborhood treasure with the talent of a special occasion spot. Inside, whitewashed brick, a living wall crafted of moss and quirky decorative elements create a contemporary ambience, while an amiable staff tends to every detail.

The cooking here is at once casual and ambitious, thanks to Chef Ryan Ratino's time spent in some cutting-edge kitchens—think minibar, for example. Here, his menu is divided into three categories, including snacks, medium plates and large plates intended for sharing.

Find a clear sense of artistry and whimsy in such dishes as the foie gras negroni, which is topped with Campari gelée and accompanied by warm madeleines. Squab and lobster united by a rich sauce Américaine turns classic surf and turf on its head; while simple yet impressively executed dishes like pappardelle with lamb ragù dazzle palates with wow-worthy flavor and agreeable prices. Strawberries and cream, where cake batter frozen in liquid nitrogen is unveiled with a dramatic cascade of cool smoke, is a dreamy way to seal this deal.

1906 14th St. NW (bet. T & U Sts.)

U St

(202) 518-7926 — **WEB:** www.brescadc.com

Dinner Tue – Sun

PRICE: $$

CAVA MEZZE ⫴○

Greek • *Neighborhood*

MAP: 4-C2

It turns out that you can be all things to all people, at least at Cava Mezze. This place manages to lure the post-work crowd who come to down drinks and talk shop. Yet this casual Greek restaurant with palatable prices is also popular among families with kids in tow.

There is a long list of shareable plates, plus seafood, meat and pasta. Additionally, quality ingredients sourced from area farms enhance simple preparations. While most of these honor the Greek standards (for instance, spanakopita is revved up by thick, creamy yogurt; and tender, buttery lamb chops are accompanied by fries), the kitchen also challenges convention. If that's not enough, it even delivers a few Med-influenced riffs—perhaps lamb sliders and orzo mac n cheese?

■ 527 8th St. SE (bet. E & G Sts.)

▦ Eastern Market

℘ (202) 543-9090 — **WEB:** www.cavamezze.com

■ Lunch & dinner daily   PRICE: $$

CENTROLINA ⫴○

Italian • *Osteria*

▢ ⊯   **MAP:** 3-A3

Located at CityCenterDC, this bright, inviting spot is part-osteria—equipped with a wood-burning oven—and part-market, offering goods like homemade pasta, pastries and coffee, to go. Inside, you'll find big windows overlooking colorful boutiques, an open kitchen, and a granite bar for sipping cocktails. The beverage program also offers a list of apertivi and Italian wines, arranged by region.

Chef Amy Brandwein's menu is divvied into categories like antipasti, pasta and large plates, many prepared in the famed oven. Think wildly delicious seafood starters like Hawaiian tuna crudo; or gently fried soft-shell crab with shishito aïoli. Dinner staples include tangles of fettuccine in a savory white Bolognese; or a young, perfectly roasted Amish chicken.

■ 974 Palmer Alley NW (at 10th St.)

▦ Metro Center

℘ (202) 898-2426 — **WEB:** www.centrolinadc.com

■ Lunch Sun – Fri Dinner nightly   PRICE: $$$

CHERCHER ⚇

Ethiopian · *Simple*

MAP: 3-A1

There are some restaurants that feed more than just an appetite and Chercher is one of them. Set on the second floor of a townhouse just outside Little Ethiopia, this tidy jewel may have the bright walls and exposed brick so often seen in mom-and-pop spots, but rest assured that it delivers more than just a spicy stew with a home-kitchen feel.

Expect authentic items native to the culturally rich region of the namesake mountains. Rip off a piece of the cool and lacy injera and then dig into the lamb wat, a tender stew fueled by the fiery notes of berbere. Simmered vegetables add a welcome dose of earthy flavor on the side, but wait, what's that over there? It's the under-the-radar and off-the-menu dishes that lure expats with bated breath.

◼ 1334 9th St. NW (bet. N & O Sts.)

🚇 Mt Vernon Sq

✆ (202) 299-9703 — **WEB:** www.chercherrestaurant.com

◼ Lunch & dinner daily   PRICE: 🍴

CHINA CHILCANO ⚇

Peruvian · *Colorful*

MAP: 3-B4

Bring a group of friends and keep the pisco coming at this José Andrés marvel, where the vibrant décor and bold, flavorful cuisine are anything but humdrum. The dining room is a feast for the eyes, featuring sky-high ceilings decked out with red glass lamps and neon lights.

Specialty ingredients from Peru find their way into many of this kitchen's dishes, and the menu brings together three major culinary influences in the country: Chinese, Japanese and Criollo. Thick and buttery slices of Ora King salmon ceviche arrive in a pool of tart yuzu juice, garnished with creamy avocado, trout roe and whole sweetie drop peppers. Meanwhile, a wonderfully seasoned stir-fry of smoky lomo saltado gets added crunch from a nest of fried potato sticks.

◼ 418 7th St. NW (bet. D & E Sts.)

🚇 Archives

✆ (202) 783-0941 — **WEB:** www.chinachilcano.com

◼ Lunch & dinner daily   PRICE: $$

CHLOE

International · Chic

&

MAP: 4-A4

After working at some of DC's most popular and dynamic kitchens, Chef Haidar Karoum ventures out with his first solo project. Tucked into the trendy Navy Yard district, Chloe's menu is eclectic and deeply personalized, seemingly built out to Haider's unique resume. The shareable plates menu gathers ingredients from across the globe, presenting them in original—and consistently delicious—ways.

Kick things off with chilled cobia crudo, pooled in a savory fish sauce, with puffed black rice, crispy shallots and creamy avocado; or delicately fried cauliflower treated to a thick drizzle of tahini, shredded mint and toasted buttery pine nuts. Follow this up with roasted Icelandic cod, cleverly crusted with papadum and set afloat in a vibrant yellow curry.

- 1331 4th St. SE (at Tingey St.)
- Navy Yard-Ballpark
- (202) 313-7007 — **WEB:** www.restaurantchloe.com
- Dinner nightly
PRICE: $$

CONVIVIAL ⅋

French · Chic

MAP: 3-B1

Truth be told, Convivial excels in all areas. It scores major points for its location, anchoring the base of City Market at O in the up-and-coming Shaw neighborhood; ranks high on style with its clean, rustic-modern aesthetic; and boasts service so downright relaxed, the servers wear jeans and sneakers. But the real reason customers keep coming back to this energetic hot spot is most certainly for the food: bold and playful takes on the tried-and-true that are made for sharing.

Popular with young professionals, families and academics from nearby Howard University, this whimsical new-meets-old menu marries French and American cuisine. Think garlicky, deep-fried escargots in a blanket, fried chicken coq au vin or Chesapeake blue catfish bouillabaisse.

- 801 O St. NW (bet. 8th & 9th Sts.)
- Mt Vernon Sq
- (202) 525-2870 — **WEB:** www.convivialdc.com
- Lunch Sat – Sun Dinner nightly
PRICE: $$

THE DABNEY ✿

American • *Rustic*

MAP: 3-A1

The Blagden Alley may have been charmless once, but it now teems with exciting culinary gems. Entering The Dabney is like finding the end of a rainbow. Inside, discover a farmhouse-chic space with an open kitchen, wood-fired oven and eclectic, well-dressed crowd.

This cuisine is suitable for anyone looking to delve into regional, Mid-Atlantic food through a menu that marries traditional and contemporary flavors. Thanks to Chef Jeremiah Langhorne's direction, diners can look forward to a supremely rich, almost buttery scallop crudo dressed with citrus, herbs and peanuts—and when that dish is finished with a shard of sheep's milk cheese, it is a reminder to expect the unexpected here. Group dining is highly recommended, so friends can maximize the number of small plates and even share a few of the mains, including the very homey chicken and dumplings. Don't miss out on desserts as they flaunt such classics as apple crumble with house-made ice cream bearing just a hint of Bourbon.

Housed nearby, The Dabney Cellar is an ideal spot to while away the waiting time before your meal. Their charcuterie and cheese vie for serious attention—not unlike the wine list of 30-some choices by the glass.

■ 122 Blagden Alley NW (bet. M & N Sts.)

▥ Mt Vernon Sq

☎ (202) 450-1015 — **WEB:** www.thedabney.com

■ Dinner Tue – Sun   **PRICE: $$**

DAIKAYA ⭐
Japanese · Simple

&

MAP: 3-B3

There are restaurants where soaking in the atmosphere is part of the experience, and then there's Daikaya. This no-reservations ramen shop is bursting at the seams (though the izakaya upstairs is an acceptable consolation prize if the wait downstairs is interminable). The unfussy space is filled with communal tables and booths, but the counter offers an unbeatable view of the hustle and bustle. Loud pop and rap music set the tone here, where you're expected to order, slurp and move on.

Daikaya is famous for its Sapporo-style ramen. Here, the white miso tare is kicked up a notch with chili spice. It's the most popular bowl, but try the special mugi-miso (barley miso) ramen with a side of citrusy yuzu kosho chili sauce for a change of pace.

◼ 705 6th St. NW (bet. G & H Sts.)
🔲 Gallery Pl-Chinatown
✆ (202) 589-1600 — **WEB:** www.daikaya.com
◼ Lunch & dinner daily

PRICE: 🍴

DAS 👻
Ethiopian · Elegant

MAP: 6-C2

Nestled inside a classic Georgetown townhouse, Das is a haven of soothing colors and lush fabrics. Great care has gone into its styling, and the warm, generous spirit of the staff ensures that the entire experience is every bit as pleasant and refined.

The impressive menu runs the gamut from traditional Ethiopian cuisine to dishes that have the potential to take even the most seasoned and ambitious palate by surprise. A basket filled with injera—a spongy and sour bread that serves as both chaser and utensil—is never-ending. For a meal that won't disappoint, order the chicken and beef combination sampler. Then use rolls of that delicious injera to dig into mouthful after flavorful mouthful of surprisingly varied textures and degrees of heat.

◼ 1201 28th St. NW (at M St.)
🔲 Foggy Bottom-GWU
✆ (202) 333-4710 — **WEB:** www.dasethiopian.com
◼ Lunch & dinner daily

PRICE: $$

DBGB KITCHEN AND BAR

French • Bistro

MAP: 3-A3

DBGB Kitchen and Bar's City Center locale may rub shoulders with the likes of Hermès and Louis Vuitton, but this light-filled French restaurant maintains a relaxed elegance with tile floors, dark wood furnishings and orb pendant lights. It's the kind of place where local politicos and dealmakers come to dish, drink and dine.

The menu is varied, with ambitious Americanized cuisine (chicken soup and yellowfin tuna) and traditional French selections sharing equal billing. Highlights include the spot-on steak tartare, delicious blue crab spaghettini and plump scallops in a well-executed and superbly buttery grenobloise. A massive burger with pork belly veers stateside, while classic roast chicken and steak frites are redolent of a Parisian bistro.

931 H St. NW (bet. 9th & 10th Sts.)
Gallery Pl-Chinatown
(202) 695-7660 — **WEB:** www.dbgb.com
Lunch & dinner daily

PRICE: $$

DEL MAR

Spanish • Chic

MAP: 4-A3

Chef Fabio Trabocchi's latest restaurant owns a stylish resort-chic vibe by way of coastal blues and whites, polished brass fixtures and large windows overlooking the channel.

Luxury ingredients find equal footing alongside classic Spanish flavor profiles, and the result is a can't-miss menu. Barely touched or simply prepared, the beautifully presented fish are a highlight, but make sure to also sample their highly sought-after seasonal tapas, as well as the curated selection of Spanish meats and cheeses. Seasonal dishes have featured asparagus blanco, a thick stalk of French asparagus, poached and served over ajo blanco. Andalusian gambas al ajillo, starring shrimp laced with garlic and chilies, are accompanied by tufts of bread for sopping.

791 Wharf St. SW (bet. 7th & 9th Sts.)
Waterfront
(202) 525-1402 — **WEB:** www.delmardc.com
Lunch Tue – Sun Dinner nightly

PRICE: $$$

THE DINER

American • *Family*

MAP: 2-A3

Nothing replaces a good diner. Where else can you tuck into a plate of bacon-wrapped meatloaf at 2:00 A.M.? The Diner is open 24/7 and its frenetic kitchen is always abuzz. Start off with a really good cup of Counter Culture coffee or if you're feeling more hair of the dog, a Bloody Mary.

It's not just standard diner fare here, where breakfast specials like bread pudding-French toast or tofu scramble with house-made salsa lean gourmet. Nursing a hangover? Straight-up comfort food is what they do best. Order the biscuit and gravy, highlighting a flaky house-made biscuit slathered in creamy sauce with sweet Italian sausage—it's a decadent way to start the day. Finally, sip on a cookies-and-cream milkshake, best enjoyed atop a red vinyl stool at the counter.

- 2453 18th St. NW (bet. Columbia & Belmont Rds.)
- Woodley Park
- (202) 232-8800 — **WEB:** www.dinerdc.com
- Lunch & dinner daily

PRICE: 🍸

DOI MOI

Asian • *Minimalist*

MAP: 2-B4

Set on a corner and flooded with sunshine, Doi Moi's interior is defined by its light, bright and mostly white modern look. Sit at the long, expansive counter facing the exhibition kitchen, or in one of two dining areas with sleek tables framed by simple blonde wood chairs.

The restaurant's interior belies the flavor-packed riot of its food. The kitchen turns out spicy and bold Southeast Asian dishes, most with a heavy Thai bent. Seared salmon in a pool of turmeric-tinged coconut milk is simply prepared but flavorful, while the pandan «ho ho» takes on the popular packaged snack cake with an Asian flair. Pandan-infused chiffon cake rolled around a coconut kaya frosting and encased in a white chocolate shell, this ho ho is anything but ho-hum.

- 1800 14th St. NW (at S St.)
- U St
- (202) 733-5131 — **WEB:** www.doimoidc.com
- Dinner nightly

PRICE: $$

DUE SOUTH
Southern • Tavern

MAP: 4-A4

Set in the Lumber Shed building smack dab in the middle of the Yards Park, Due South is bright and airy with high ceilings and walls of windows. But the wraparound patio with its stellar views of the park and river is the place to be.

This kitchen's compass certainly points south and smoked meats are ever-present, but there's nothing simple about their prettied-up Southern-style cooking, enhanced with seasonal produce. Kale and heirloom tomatoes take the lead out of typically heavy shrimp and grits, while the Brunswick stew is particularly flavorful. If the hanger steak with broccoli rabe feels a little too—well, northern—take refuge in a slice of pie or cobbler. Beers by the draft or bottle are plentiful, but check the rotating list of specialty brews.

🔲 301 Water St. SE (at 3rd St.)

🚇 Navy Yard-Ballpark

✆ (202) 479-4616 — **WEB:** www.duesouthdc.com

🔲 Lunch & dinner daily

PRICE: $$

EATBAR
Gastropub • Tavern

MAP: 4-C2

Where do you go when you want to throw back a few beers, listen to good tunes and catch up with pals? Eatbar. This casual spot is like your living room, only with better food (and a way-cool jukebox). It's all about the sharing economy here, where small plates rule the roost. The beer list is vast and the wine selection surprises with lesser known finds.

Small-batch charcuterie and whole animal butchery are passions of the chef, so the menu is meat-driven, but right sizing keeps portions in check. The carte is whimsically categorized so while "bready things" bring a summer tomato tartine with ricotta, "beasty things" unveil a cotechino burger enriched with tomato aïoli and melted cheese. Seal the deal with "sweet things" like lemon-scented ricotta donuts.

🔲 415 8th St. SE (bet. D & E Sts.)

🚇 Eastern Market

✆ (202) 847-4827 — **WEB:** www.eat-bar.com

🔲 Lunch Sat – Sun Dinner nightly

PRICE: $$

ELLĒ

Contemporary · Neighborhood

MAP: 2-B1

This indie hot spot with a retro-chic décor and cool staff has so many things going for it. First, there's the team behind it, who've already struck gold on the city's dining scene. Then there's the location, inside the former Heller's Bakery, which was an 80-year-old neighborhood institution. And finally, there's the food. This all-day kitchen churns out tempting baked goods in the morning, quiches and sandwiches at lunch and a full dinner carte in the evening. Slather nori butter on excellent house-made country bread before diving into black pepper spaetzle studded with littleneck clams, tossed in a garlic and butter sauce.

Don't skimp on dessert as it's a sacrilege in these hallowed bakery halls. Fluffy and tangy goat cheese-cheesecake is a great pick.

▪ 3221 Mt. Pleasant St. NW (bet. Lamont St. & Park Rd.)
▪ Columbia Heights
✆ (202) 652-0040 — **WEB:** www.eatatelle.com
▪ Lunch daily Dinner Wed – Mon   PRICE: $$

ESPITA MEZCALERIA

Mexican · Rustic

MAP: 3-A1

The name is the first sign that this place takes its mezcal seriously. Step inside only to find that dark woods, concrete floors and steel accents all work to create an industrial vibe. Shelves are lined with the elixir, whose selection is eye-popping to say the least. In fact, there are certified master mezcaliers on staff, so prepare to go in late tomorrow and kick back with a flight. That said, Espita Mezcaleria is so much more than just a watering hole.

This kitchen turns out tasty Southern Mexican items—think tortas, tacos and seven types of delicious, house-made moles. Tender, shredded short rib-topped griddled sopes are moist and nutty, while the flaky grilled tilapia-packed tacos drizzled with a creamy chipotle-mayo are...one word...sensational.

▪ 1250 9th St. NW (at N St.)
▪ Mt Vernon Sq
✆ (202) 621-9695 — **WEB:** www.espitadc.com
▪ Lunch Sat- Sun Dinner nightly   PRICE: $$

ESTADIO

Spanish • Rustic

MAP: 1-D1

With its stone-accented walls, chunky wood furnishings and poured concrete bar studded with Moorish tile, Estadio, or "stadium" as it translates, plays up its Spanish influences. It's no surprise then that the focus is on tapas, but these unusual combinations and preparations offer a pleasant twist on tradition.

Golden-brown jamón croquetas are amped up with pickled cucumber; fava bean and almond spread is a thick and creamy snack; and sizzling squid a la plancha is drizzled with a citrusy salsa verde. Chase it all down with a glass of wine from Spain, Portugal and the Canary Islands; a cocktail mixed with house-made tonics; or even a slushito—an icy blend of grapefruit, Bourbon and amontillado, designed to counteract a hot summer's night.

 1520 14th St. NW (at Church St.)

(202) 319-1404 — **WEB:** www.estadio-dc.com

Lunch Fri – Sun Dinner nightly   **PRICE:** $$

ETETE

Ethiopian • Contemporary décor

MAP: 2-C4

Decked out in walls finished with elegant gold and furnished with plush banquettes, Etete is definitely not your grad student's Ethiopian standard. In fact, if this setting makes eating with your hands seem slightly out of place, you'll get over it as soon as those intense flavors hit your lips.

This talented kitchen delivers appealing and well-seasoned cooking that celebrates tradition while incorporating fresh and new influences. Awaze beef tibs, for instance, slowly simmered with spices and served with yellow split peas (yemisir alicha) are a nod to the past; while injera "tacos" with berbere chicken, ayib farmer's cheese and collard greens; or crispy green lentil rolls with a Horn spice-balsamic reduction both smack of contemporary nuances.

1942 9th St. NW (bet. T & U Sts.)

U St

(202) 232-7600 — **WEB:** www.eteterestaurant.com

Lunch & dinner daily   **PRICE:** $$

ETHIOPIC

Ethiopian · Simple

MAP: 8-A4

With its large windows, bustling energy and brightly hued interior, Ethiopic is an ideal fit for the melting pot that is H Street. Though minimalist, the dining room's bare tables are juxtaposed with pops of color from decorative wall hangings and other artwork.

This family-run spot turns out classic, well-made dishes with complex flavors, and the menu is a veritable treasure trove for vegetarians. Tibs, a marinated beef or lamb dish served with sautéed vegetables, delivers a kick of heat; while the slowly simmered beef in the sega key wot proves that good things do come to those who wait. Of course, everything comes with the obligatory injera, thicker here than usual, and no meal is complete without a cup of that seriously rich Ethiopian coffee.

- ◼ 401 H St. NE (at 4th St.)
- 🚇 Union Station
- ✆ (202) 675-2066 — **WEB:** www.ethiopicrestaurant.com
- ◼ Lunch Fri – Sun Dinner Tue – Sun   **PRICE:** $$

FANCY RADISH 😀

Vegan · Trendy

♿

MAP: 8-A4

The power couple behind Philly's Vedge has brought their haute cuisine approach to vegan cooking in the nation's capital with Fancy Radish. Set at the base of an urbane condo building, this industrial-chic space is perpetually buzzing with locals.

While these dishes may be defined by what they lack—namely meat, cheese or butter—the experience here is all about what you're getting (not what you're missing). Razor-thin trumpet mushrooms are a clever stand-in for pasta, bathed with a silky broth; while spicy dan dan noodles are tossed with a tahini-based sauce for a creamy, savory bite. This kitchen keeps you on your toes through dessert—when hearty chickpea-flour donuts are adeptly paired with a rhubarb- and sour cherry-gazpacho for a well-deserved bow.

- ◼ 600 H St. NE (bet. 6th & 7th Sts.)
- ✆ (202) 675-8341 — **WEB:** www.fancyradishdc.com
- ◼ Dinner Tue – Sun   **PRICE:** $$

FIOLA ✿

Italian • *Elegant*

🍇 ⚬ 🏠 ⬜ 🖐

MAP: 3-B4

Polished and professional with an upscale setting made for brokering deals, Fiola is just what the politician ordered. Its central location near the Archives makes it a go-to for the power crowd, and the bar is perfect for blowing off steam after a busy day of debating.

Thanks to truly sophisticated cuisine, the somewhat stiff environs and overly scripted service staff are soon forgiven. And despite its traditional demeanor, the menu actually allows for flexibility with the ability to craft your own four- and five-course meals in addition to a grand tasting menu. The chef's cooking style is both ultra-luxurious and Italian-influenced, with a highly stylized bent to boot. Meals may begin with a single jumbo stalk of white asparagus, dressed with black truffle vinaigrette and caviar, before moving on to hay-smoked potato gnocchi, presented with flair under a glass cloche. Wild turbot with chunks of razor clams and fava beans is also shielded within a glass cloche, though this excellent dish impresses with its rich flavors alone.

As for the wine list? As one would expect, it's showy, littered with big names and curated for those with sizeable expense accounts and companions to impress.

🟦 601 Pennsylvania Ave. NW (entrance on Indiana Ave.)

🏛 Archives

✆ (202) 628-2888 — **WEB:** www.fioladc.com

🟦 Lunch Mon – Fri Dinner nightly

PRICE: $$$$

FIOLA MARE

Seafood • Elegant

MAP: 6-B3

The husband-and-wife duo behind some of this city's hottest restaurants has a stunner on their hands with Fiola Mare. Hugging the Potomac River with unparalleled views, it may be difficult to find a more beautiful setting in town. Of course, those lovely sights come at a price, so expect a bill more palatable to the expense-account type. Still, the wonderfully charming waitstaff coddles everyone.

Italian-leaning seafood is this kitchen's dictum. A plump Capital oyster floating in a zabaglione of prosecco and topped with Kaviari caviar is likely to cause sticker-shock, but it is a particular standout. The squid-ink bucatini leaves an intense impression, while pesce intero del giorno—which is deboned tableside—makes for a great signature and show.

▨ 3050 K St. NW, Ste. 101 (at 31st St.)

▣ Foggy Bottom-GWU

✆ (202) 628-0065 — **WEB:** www.fiolamaredc.com

▨ Lunch Tue – Sun Dinner nightly   **PRICE: $$$$**

GARRISON

American • Neighborhood

MAP: 4-C2

Despite the heavy competition in its bustling Barracks Row location, Garrison stands apart with farm-fresh food and modern-rustic good looks. The brick patio, lined with flowering plants and aromatic herbs, makes a good first impression, and heat lamps extend the life of alfresco dining. Inside, abundant wood defines the look, which subscribes to the Scandinavian, less-is-more school of thought.

Area farms dictate the menu, but for hyper-seasonal selections, note the handwritten daily specials. The cooking style is ramped up American: smoke-infused potatoes are balanced by a pungent ramp aïoli; and green chickpea-crusted Chesapeake blue catfish is matched with a rhubarb coulis. Strawberry short cake parfait is like springtime in a glass.

▨ 524 8th St. SE (bet. E & G Sts.)

▣ Eastern Market

✆ (202) 506-2445 — **WEB:** www.garrisondc.com

▨ Lunch Sun Dinner Tue – Sun   **PRICE: $$**

GHIBELLINA ▮◍

Italian • *Trattoria*

  ♿ ⛱ 🛏

MAP: 1-D1

Ghibellina's marble bar is a favorite hangout, but don't let the cocktail-swilling patrons steer you away, since this kitchen gives its bar a serious run. Dark wood floors, iron accents and exposed brick are a nod to the Old World, while the front sidewalk patio is a top people-watching spot.

Lunch is largely focused on salads and knockout pizzas. Ramp pizza reveals a delightful interplay between zingy, garlicky-onion ramps and creamy cheeses, including crumbled ricotta and fior di latte. Dinner expands to include antipasti, pastas (like bucatini alle vongole) and mains (like pollo al mattone or chicken under a brick). It's a linger-a-little-longer kind of place, so order dessert. The affogato al caffe's gelato with robust espresso is a nice finish.

  ▢ 1610 14th St. NW (bet. Corcoran & Q Sts.)
  ▣ U St
  𝒞 (202) 803-2389 — **WEB:** www.ghibellina.com
  ▢ Lunch Fri – Sun Dinner nightly   PRICE: $$

HANK'S OYSTER BAR ▮◍

Seafood • *Neighborhood*

  ♿ ⛱ 🛏

MAP: 1-C1

The original of four locations, Hank's Oyster Bar promises a good time and a full stomach. Snag a seat on the spacious front patio or opt for a table indoors where bottles of malt vinegar and Old Bay seasoning are a sign of things to come.

Meals begin with a bowl of humble Goldfish cheese crackers. Then prepare yourself for a sea, ahem, of dishes. Feast on platters of raw bar beauties to bowls of steaming chowder to oysters any way you want 'em (Hog Island style involves dunking in a tangy lemon-garlic-Tabasco-butter sauce, a sprinkling of breadcrumbs and shredded cheese and broiling until caramelized!). Of course, lobster rolls and crab cake sandwiches with Old Bay-seasoned fries are positively Proustian, conjuring up days at the beach from years past.

  ▢ 1624 Q St. NW (bet. 16th & 17th Sts.)
  ▣ Dupont Circle
  𝒞 (202) 462-4265 — **WEB:** www.hanksoysterbar.com
  ▢ Lunch & dinner daily   PRICE: $$

HAZEL

Fusion • *Contemporary décor*

MAP: 2-C4

Tucked into DC's hip Shaw neighborhood, this charmer is low-lit and cozy by evening, with Sunday brunch offering a brighter ambience care of jumbo windows and an outdoor patio. Dishes are a mash-up of ingredients from around the world, tied together with an East Asian slant—a vision deftly translated by a kitchen skilled enough to weave disparate ingredients into a fun, cohesive menu.

The shareable plates are divided into simple categories: vegetables, breads, fish and meat. Crispy tofu arrives perfectly creamy in the center, topped with a shiitake mushroom sauce and Sichuan pepper; while succulent cuttlefish bokkeum is stir-fried with pickled green onion, charred scallion and spirals of carrots, then laced with a Korean red pepper glaze.

- 808 V St. NW (bet. 8th & 9th Sts.)
- Shaw-Howard U
- (202) 847-4980 — **WEB:** www.hazelrestaurant.com
- Lunch Sun Dinner nightly   **PRICE:** $$

HIMITSU 🍴

Asian • *Cozy*

MAP: 2-C1

Take a small space, cool staff plus a wildly creative kitchen and what do you get? Himitsu, naturally. Perhaps it should come as no surprise that it continues to garner so much buzz as it is exceedingly more fun than your average spot, and ergo, another notch in the belt of DC's dining scene.

Don't bother Googling—there is no phone and they don't take reservations. Lines form long before the door opens, but if you're lucky (or patient) enough to snag a seat at the bar or one of the snug tables, you'll find a fun, inventive menu that takes inspiration from, well, everywhere, but has an Asian bent. Think bowls of silky congee and Japanese eggplant dressed in a chili-lime vinaigrette. Charred carrots on a bed of creamy robiolina are outrageously good.

- 828 Upshur St. NW (bet. 8th & 9th Sts.)
- N/A — **WEB:** www.himitsudc.com
- Dinner Tue – Sat   **PRICE:** $$

HONEYSUCKLE

American · *Colorful*

MAP: 1-B2

Planted in Vidalia's original home turf and run by an alum of the onion-monikered restaurant, it's safe to say Honeysuckle is all about keeping it in the family—and that's a good thing. Inside, bold touches include artwork inspired by the chef's tattoos, while white tablecloths prevent it from looking too trendy.

Tuck into the bread basket, a delicious gesture filled with a buttery roll studded with ham and cheddar cheese; sweet zucchini bread; and a hearty beer roll. The menu leans American, but the chef's love affair with all things Nordic means items such as slow-roasted Icelandic cod are worth ordering. Veal sweetbreads tucked inside a pastry shell and finished with a béarnaise pudding sauce are decidedly delicious—if a touch decadent.

▨ 1990 M St. NW (bet. 19th & 20th Sts.)

▨ Farragut North

✆ (202) 659-1990 — **WEB:** www.honeysuckledc.com

▨ Lunch Mon – Fri Dinner nightly   PRICE: $$$

INDIGO

Indian · *Simple*

MAP: 8-A3

It's yellow, not the telltale blue of its name, that defines this sunny Indian restaurant. Located in a cheerful house with a patio full of colorful picnic tables, Indigo is far from fancy (it's largely self-service and food is served in disposable containers). But, how can you not adore a place where love notes from customers cover the walls?

Indian expats and residents line up for such classic comfort cooking from the sub-continent as as spicy chicken masala and tender, melt-in-your-mouth goat curry. Even side dishes are elevated here—for instance, daal is packed with smoky flavor and doused in a cardamom-scented sauce, while paneer paratha (flatbread stuffed with cheese, onion, chopped red chilies and cilantro) is especially fluffy and addictive.

▨ 243 K St. NE (at 3rd St.)

▨ NoMa-Gallaudet U

✆ (202) 544-4777 — **WEB:** www.indigowdc.com

▨ Lunch Mon – Fri Dinner Mon – Sat   PRICE: ⊜⊜

INDIQUE

Indian · *Colorful*

                                                        MAP: 5-C1

This bi-level beauty isn't afraid of making a splash—envision brightly painted walls hung with Indian-themed art, as well as colorful cushions that add a dose of serotonin.

The cooking oscillates between classic and contemporary, but this kitchen truly shines at night when the chef shares favorites from his Indian hometown. Start things off right with samosa chaat tossing those potato-and-pea crispy delights with curried chickpeas, a sweet tamarind sauce and spicy cilantro-chili chutney. Cooked in a tandoor, chicken tikka makhani is then bathed in a tomato- and caramelized-onion gravy, scented with fenugreek and spiced up with ginger. Paneer pasanda is beloved by vegetarians, but for an old-meets-new triumph, go for the cauliflower-pecorino kulchas.

■ 3512-14 Connecticut Ave. NW (bet. Ordway & Porter Sts.)

■ Cleveland Park

✆ (202) 244-6600 — **WEB:** www.indique.com

■ Lunch Fri – Sun Dinner nightly   PRICE: $$

IRON GATE

Mediterranean · *Romantic*

                                                          MAP: 1-C2

Blessed with one of the coolest dining spaces in the city (a former stable and carriageway tucked inside a historic townhouse), Iron Gate has a good thing going even before you take your first bite. Its cozy dining room features rustic dark wood beams, sleek leather banquettes and a roaring fireplace; while out back, a lovely—and lively—trellised garden patio stays heated and open nearly year-round.

The good news is the food is just as exceptional—dinner features an à la carte menu with dishes that meander between Greek, Italian and Mediterranean flavors. Sesame-crusted feta finds perfect harmony in sweet and tart vin cotto and honey; while caramelized ricotta gnocchi gets a leg up from pork sausage ragù, chili pepper and a dusting of parmesan.

■ 1734 N St. NW (bet. 17th & 18th Sts.)

■ Dupont Circle

✆ (202) 524-5202 — **WEB:** www.irongaterestaurantdc.com

■ Lunch Tue – Sun Dinner nightly   PRICE: $$$

THE INN AT LITTLE WASHINGTON ✿✿✿

American • Elegant

MAP: N/A

Set 90 minutes from DC in a town whose very existence seems tied to the restaurant, The Inn at Little Washington is a destination in every sense of the word. Embellished to the last inch, the dining room resembles a jewelry box lined with patterned carpets, lush wallpaper, heavy drapes and bejeweled upholstery. Servers are knowledgeable and warm; the room is conducive to conversations. This is a civilized affair for sophisticated patrons celebrating a special occasion.

The restaurant may be 40 years old, but Chef Patrick O'Connell's cuisine shines as brightly as ever. The three menus each have a unique focus: "Enduring Classics" are updated signatures; "Gastronaut" reflects the kitchen's ambitions; and "The Good Earth" offers superb vegetarian items. Guests can also traipse through all three for a full sense of what this kitchen can do. Their extraordinary focus on detail and sourcing is clear from the start in the BLT-inspired amuse-bouche with heirloom tomato gelée, or the excellent rye bread smeared with honeycomb butter. Sauces work a particular magic, as seen in the truffle-infused tartar with morel "crabcake."

Desserts like coconut sorbet with ginger granité are perfection.

◻ 309 Middle St. (Washington, VA)

✆ (540) 675-3800 — **WEB:** www.theinnatlittlewashington.com

◻ Dinner Wed – Mon   **PRICE: $$$$**

IVY CITY SMOKEHOUSE

Seafood • Tavern

MAP: 8-C1

Lucky are the eaters who make their way to this unique seafood smokehouse. Inside the warehouse-like space, a daily market and state-of-the-art smokehouse reside at street level. Above this, find a tavern-like restaurant with a large, open-air rooftop. The fish is fresh, the staff is super-friendly and the vibe is irresistible with occasional live music.

A platter offers a broad sample of artisanal smoked goodies, like Indian candy (a sweet, salty and almost jerk-like smoked salmon); glistening, coral-pink smoked salmon; pepper-smoked salmon embedded with crushed peppercorns; and an impossibly good whitefish salad. Don't miss the chalkboard's daily specials, like tender crab cake so flaky and minimally dressed you'll think you're seaside.

■ 1356 Okie St. NE (at Fenwick St.)
℘ (202) 529-3300 — **WEB:** www.ivycitysmokehouse.com
■ Lunch Tue – Sun Dinner nightly   PRICE: $$

IZAKAYA SEKI ⅈ◯

Japanese • Minimalist

MAP: 2-C4

Set within a two-level townhouse in a residential area, Izakaya Seki delivers a simple, yet spot-on experience. With just 40 seats and a no-reservation policy, you may have to wait for your seat—either at the sushi bar on the first floor or upstairs where exposed beams and shelves lined with sake bottles make for a Kyoto-chic ambience.

The father-daughter team ventures beyond sushi and sashimi to impress diners with authentic Japanese dishes, and it is evident the chef loves what he does. Ojiya soba, lovingly prepared in Japan and dried outdoors for one year before being stirred into the dashi and topped with sweet, flavorful pork belly, is nothing if not memorable. And delicate baby octopus braised in sake and mirin is sweet, salty and just a bit smoky.

■ 1117 V St. NW (bet. 11th & 12th Sts.)
Ⓜ U St
℘ (202) 588-5841 — **WEB:** www.sekidc.com
■ Dinner Tue – Sun   PRICE: $$

JACK ROSE DINING SALOON

American • *Tavern*

MAP: 2-A4

What can brown do for you? If you're Jack Rose, a whole lot. Brown liquor is revered here, where four walls are lined with shelves of the stuff. There are 2,500 bottles and there is even a library-style, rolling wall-mounted ladder to access them. Don't worry if your head spins before you take a sip; a Scotch specialist on the premises is happy to offer advice.

Jack Rose isn't just about the bar; the kitchen delivers a hit list of gastropub-style eats. Dandelion greens pesto atop chewy fettucine is creative and flavorful; fried quail served over toast and spread with creamy sawmill gravy studded with sausage crumbles is positively delicious; and a warm mini butter cake topped with a scoop of butter-pecan ice cream is as tasty as it is adorable.

 2007 18th St. NW (bet. California & Vernon Sts.)

U St

(202) 588-7388 — **WEB:** www.jackrosediningsaloon.com

Dinner nightly   **PRICE:** $$

JALEO

Spanish • *Colorful*

MAP: 3-B4

It's impossible to be glum at Jaleo. This Spanish jewel is unafraid of color and pattern, and flaunts such decorative accents as mounted bear trophies and convoluted art installations. Of course, that table you're eating on doubles as a foosball table for a lively duel in between courses.

Cocktails are enticing, so sip on the magic mojito strained over cotton candy. The mood may be fun, but the food is seriously good (this is a José Andrés venture, after all). Some of the standouts from this kitchen are the simplest—a white bean salad tailed by the razor-thin crust of the pan de cristal con tomate. But don't forget about that jamón—the 48-month cured jamón ibérico de Bellota is not to be missed. The hits keep coming here, so save room for a bit of sweet.

480 7th St. NW (at E St.)

Gallery Pl-Chinatown

(202) 628-7949 — **WEB:** www.jaleo.com

Lunch & dinner daily   **PRICE:** $$

JOSELITO'S CASA DE COMIDAS 🍴

Spanish • Contemporary décor

♿ 🍴 ⬚ 🛋️   **MAP:** 4-B1

Pull up a chair at this intimate restaurant where portraits line the walls and everyone feels like family. Joselito's offers a spectrum of appealing Spanish favorites that are doled out with extra love. In fact, this kitchen even encourages you to order based on your appetite: go for the tapa portion to sample a wide variety or commit to a larger portion if you've spent the morning spinning.

These talented chefs aren't forging a new path; instead, they're cooking only with the most top-notch ingredients and tender, loving care. Start things off with the velvety smooth chicken liver terrine before tucking in to the creamy delicious "pasta" topped with jumbo crab, sea urchin, pimiento and shrimp. Finish with sopa de chocolate blanco for a decadent treat.

▪ 660 Pennsylvania Ave. SE (at 7th St.)
✆ (202) 930-6955 — **WEB:** www.joselitodc.com
▪ Lunch & dinner daily   PRICE: $$

KAFE LEOPOLD 🍴

Austrian • Contemporary décor

🍴 🛋️ 🛋️   **MAP:** 6-A2

Kafe Leopold (+ Konditorei) is the exact antidote to those too-cute-for-words pastry shops. Sure, there may be 26 different desserts to tempt your sweet tooth here, but there's nothing twee about this sleek space tucked in an alley behind posh M Street. Descend the stairs and discover a lovely courtyard garden—complete with a trickling fountain—before stepping into a relaxed arena with eye-catching photos and a decidedly modern ambience.

Savory choices include rostbraten vom Angusrind and bratwurst, but even with their delicious homemade taste, it's the final course that is first priority. Peruse the long list of Kaffeespezialitäten, and then nibble on a slice of esterhazy (five-layer hazelnut cake), a delicious éclair or any other can't-go-wrong treat.

▪ 3315 M St. NW
✆ (202) 965-6005 — **WEB:** www.kafeleopolds.com
▪ Lunch & dinner daily   PRICE: $$

KALIWA

Asian · Design

MAP: 4-A3

If you cannot make a trip to Thailand, or the Philippines just isn't in this year's budget, you're in for a treat. A dinner at Kaliwa, tucked inside the District Wharf, is not just a consolation prize. It's a true feast, about as delicious as can be imagined outside of a journey across the world.

Chef Cathal Armstrong's authentic and delicious Korean, Filipino or Thai cooking is blessed with serious flavor. From the Filipino column, a classic pancit gets some elevated polish with crisp, sweet spring peas, spaghetti-like ribbons of carrots, crunchy chicharrónes and a tangle of tender noodles. From the Thai menu, dishes like the pad tua faak yaow and kaeng daeng don't just bring the spice, but showcase each complex ingredient in perfect, sublime harmony.

751 Wharf St. SW (bet. 7th & 9th Sts.)
Waterfront-SEU Station
(202) 516-4739 — **WEB:** www.kaliwadc.com
Lunch & dinner daily

PRICE: $$

KAPNOS

Greek · Mediterranean décor

MAP: 2-B3

Nothing is lost in translation here, as this outpost is just one among a handful in town. From terra-cotta and Greek tiles to light fixtures crafted from bottles, Kapnos nails the classic taverna effect. And with two rotating, wood-fired grills, it clearly has a menu to match. This kitchen is all about the classics—roasted chicken, lamb and pork. Reserve a seat at the "chef counter" and you'll see these spits in action, churning out the likes of stone-baked flatbreads and seafood dishes. But any good Greek restaurant worth its sea salt is about sharing, so expect a long and varied mezze selection.

Quench this savory feast with a spiked lemonade on tap at the bar, which also happens to make a nice perch for solo diners wanting in on the fun.

2201 14th St. NW (at W St.)
U St
(202) 234-5000 — **WEB:** www.kapnosdc.com
Lunch Sat – Sun Dinner nightly

PRICE: $$

KARMA MODERN INDIAN

Indian · *Contemporary décor*

MAP: 3-B2

Soaring ceilings, large windows and a pleasing navy-and-white palette set a distinctly modern tone for the appropriately named Karma Modern Indian. This is a far cry from your everyday curry house as a great deal of care is taken to coax each dish with enticing flavors. Spices are ground on the premises—read about their health benefits in the thoughtful guide on the back of the menu while you wait.

The chef-driven menu is at once traditional and contemporary. Lentil salad atop paper-thin cucumber slices is a visual showstopper, while turnip goat, slow cooked with a complex sauce that is equally sweet and spicy, is outstanding. Lobster masala with green and red peppers and beetroot poriyal display the kitchen's dedication to an old-meets-new sensibility.

611 I St. NW (bet. 6th & 7th Sts.)
Gallery Pl-Chinatown
☎ (202) 898-0393 — **WEB:** www.karmamodernindian.com
Lunch & dinner daily   **PRICE:** $$$

KEREN

Ethiopian · *Simple*

MAP: 2-A4

Go ahead and order breakfast all day long, since Keren keeps the morning meal front and center. However, before you show up expecting bacon and eggs, take a second look as this is a showpiece of Eritrean cuisine. The East African nation was once occupied by Italy, and this history continues to be an influential force on its cuisine—with many pasta-centric dishes popping up on the menu. A loyal crowd alternates between watching soccer, debating Eritrean politics and filling up on the sizable portions.

Ful, a staple breakfast dish of favas, jalapeño, tomato and onion, is a good place to start (there are six variations). Then go for the "five Eritrean" items for a well-rounded, veg-focused combo that's so good it will render you unable to pick a favorite.

1780 Florida Ave. NW (bet. 18th & U Sts.)
U St
☎ (202) 265-5764 — **WEB:** N/A
Lunch & dinner daily   **PRICE:** ⊜

KINSHIP ✿

Contemporary · Design

Kinship is a prominent fixture in DC's culinary scene, thanks to Chef Eric Ziebold and wife/partner Célia Laurent's inspired cuisine. They have earned a devoted following of urbane gastronomes and locals who gladly dress to dine here, making it feel like more of an occasion.

The location across from The Walter E. Washington Convention Center belies its style, which is airy and sophisticated. In addition to Métier downstairs, the three-part space comprises a book-lined and fireplace-warmed lounge, lively bar and minimalist-chic dining room, all crafted by local designer, Darryl Carter.

The à la carte isn't just a laundry list of offerings; it's a peek inside Chef Ziebold's heart and mind. While selections from the "Ingredients" and "Indulgence" categories need no explanation, "Craft" items honor tradition and "History" selections pay tribute to sentimental favorites. Pick and choose from the different themes for a bespoke tasting menu of veal paupiette, folded with a purée of cardoons and braised in a rich veal stock. Diners are encouraged to save the best for last, with desserts like an Opéra cake, presented as a layered square of light and dark chocolate cake, mousse and almond feuilletine.

■ 1015 7th St. NW (bet. L St. & New York Ave.)
🚇 Mt Vernon Sq
✆ (202) 737-7700 — WEB: www.kinshipdc.com
■ Dinner nightly   PRICE: $$$

KITH/KIN

Contemporary · Design

MAP: 4-A3

Set within the InterContinental at the Wharf, Kith/Kin boasts towering ceilings, floods of sunlight and fabulous water views. But it isn't just about good looks here—the kitchen offers a bevy of surprises via West African, Caribbean and Creole influences. Of course, Chef Kwame Onwuachi has trained at some of the country's top restaurants, so expect nothing but special flavors and precise techniques.

Charcuterie turns tradition on its head with berbere chicharrónes and jerk duck prosciutto. Smoked redfish pâté and andouille sausage over toast is another highlight. For dessert, roasted, seedless (and heatless) habanada peppers are filled with its own mousse and served with elderflower granité, thereby proving that these unique dishes demand your attention.

801 Wharf St. SW (bet. 7th & 9th Sts.)

(202) 878-8566 — **WEB:** www.kithandkindc.com

Lunch & dinner daily
PRICE: $$$

KYIRISAN

Fusion · Trendy

MAP: 2-C4

The Ma family's heart and soul is in this Shaw gem. It's hip, yet family-friendly, and a mix of locals, tourists and political suits packs this energetic space.

Rabbit rillettes sandwiched between fried green tomato-turnip cakes drizzled with salted plum sriracha and sesame-soy sauce show off Chef Tim Ma's confirmed trademark blend of French-tinged Asian-flavored cooking. Sous vide duck confit is a clear winner, where moist, tender duck is sweet, smoky and salty; balanced by caramelized Brussels sprouts; and finally offset by a tangy apple cider gastrique. One word—irresistible! All good things must come to an end, but definitely order the matcha pavlova, a matcha meringue served with black sesame-flavored whipped cream for a nutty, not-too-sweet finale.

1924 8th St. NW (at Florida Ave.)

Shaw-Howard U

(202) 525-2383 — **WEB:** www.kyirisandc.com

Dinner nightly
PRICE: $$

KOMI ✿

Mediterranean • Chic

✿

Climb the stairs of a historic Dupont Circle townhouse to find this diminutive restaurant with a focus on drama. The smattering of well-spaced tables and a hushed ambience fashion a very promising date night. Photos are verboten, which is no matter since you're so busy having a good time in "real" time.

The staff is relaxed, engaged, and professional. That said, they provide precious little information on how each evening's single prix-fixe will unfold—there are no menus, and diners have a minimal glimpse of what is to come next. But relinquishing control to these capable chefs (and sommelier) is the only way to go, as the results are bound to leave you feeling uplifted.

Meals begin with small bites that treat the palate to raw, cool and cooked flavors. These have included soft brioche topped with trout roe, sliced sea scallop crudo over a lobster reduction and sweet-savory warm Medjool dates filled with mascarpone and finished with a sprinkle of sea salt. From there, delve into a duo of wonderfully rustic house-made pastas, like ravioli filled with celery root and dressed with morels, favas and bits of lamb's tongue. Roasted kid goat with fluffy pita conjures the best of Greece.

▨ 1509 17th St. NW (bet. P & Q Sts.)

▣ Dupont Circle

✆ (202) 332-9200 — **WEB:** www.komirestaurant.com

▨ Dinner Tue – Sat PRICE: $$$$

LA CHAUMIÈRE
French • *Bistro*

MAP: 6-C2

It may be located on a bustling Georgetown street lined with modern stores and coffee houses, but La Chaumière is as old-world as it gets—much to the delight of its loyal crowd of wealthy regulars and movers and shakers. Adorned with antique farm tools, repurposed barn wood beams and a roaring fireplace, the dining room is both charming and cozy.

Even if the interior doesn't have you at bonjour, the food—rustic and unpretentious classics such as escargot and steak frites—will do the trick. House specials include the boudin blanc, quenelles de Brochet and tripe stew. Of course, cassoulet is yet another house favorite. They've also managed to sneak in a few newcomers, like Maryland crab cakes, but you'll find even these are cleverly Frenchified.

■ 2813 M St. NW (bet. 28th & 29th Sts.)
℘ (202) 338-1784 — **WEB:** www.lachaumieredc.com
■ Lunch Mon – Fri Dinner Mon – Sat   PRICE: $$

LAPIS
Afghan • *Bistro*

MAP: 2-A3

Lapis-colored columns set against whitewashed walls set the tone for a restaurant that gleams like its namesake jewel. From the stunning Afghan rugs warming the floor to the sepia-toned heirloom photos on the walls, this place exudes warmth and charm, albeit in a highly stylish manner.

Husband-and-wife owners Zubair and Shamim Popal share the fragrant cuisine of their native Afghanistan. Light and fresh without the heavy-handed spicing of other regional cuisines, this food is a delicious discovery. Split pea soup may sound basic but here it is layered with flavor. And chopawn is the real deal—this trio of grilled-to-perfection lamb chops is served with sensational cardamom-scented rice and draws you in forkful after fluffy forkful.

■ 1847 Columbia Rd. NW (at Mintwood Pl.)
℘ (202) 299-9630 — **WEB:** www.lapisdc.com
■ Lunch Sat – Sun Dinner nightly   PRICE: $$

LE CHAT NOIR 🍴○

French • Bistro

🛋

MAP: N/A

Friendship Heights' residents are lucky indeed, as the perfect French bistro—Le Chat Noir—is nestled within their quaint neighborhood. This darling spot embodies the ideal "corner" bistro with its inviting and warm ambience and classic French cooking. It's not cutting edge, but with a panoply of French hits, who cares?

Pissaladière, typically prepared with flatbread, is literally puffed up here by way of a flaky pastry topped with caramelized onion, herbes de Provence, anchovies and green olives for Mediterranean flavor. Savor the terrific broth of the bouillabaisse before tucking into the merguez aux lentilles, two thin sausage links served with green lentils set atop a salad. Savory and sweet crêpes are a mainstay of this menu, and brunch is superb.

▪ 4907 Wisconsin Ave. NW (bet. Ellicott St. & Emery Pl.)
℘ (202) 244-2044 — **WEB:** www.lechatnoirrestaurant.com
▪ Lunch & dinner daily   **PRICE:** $$

LE DIPLOMATE 🍴○

French • Brasserie

♿ � 🛋

MAP: 1-D1

Stephen Starr takes on the nation's capital with Le Diplomate, his pitch-perfect rendition of a Rive Gauche bistro. From the shiny and large brass windows to the zinc bar and the mosaic-tiled floor, it is all très Français.

Bread lovers rejoice; there is a paean to the crusty stuff at the entrance, where ficelle-filled bags and assorted loaves and rounds are lovingly displayed. This is straightforward traditional bistro food at its best: steak tartare, croque monsieur, steak frites with sauce béarnaise and out-of-this-world moules frites. Steamed with Pernod and served marinière-style, the mussels would be succulent enough on their own, but toss in a handful of those crispy pommes frites as well as a basket of freshly sliced baguette and mon dieu!

▪ 1601 14th St. NW (at Q St.)
🚇 U St
℘ (202) 332-3333 — **WEB:** www.lediplomatedc.com
▪ Lunch Sat – Sun Dinner nightly   **PRICE:** $$

LITTLE SEROW ꭑꝋ

Thai • *Trendy*

MAP: 1-C1

It's very black-and-white at Little Serow, a spot that's neither fancy nor fussy and a stickler for rules. For starters, there's no phone, so you can forget about reservations. The menu is fixed, and that means no changes (nope, not even for your lactose-free, gluten-free, pork-hating friend). Want more spice? Don't even try to tell them how to cook. Still interested? You'd better get in line, because the door opens promptly at 5:30 P.M.

Little Serow lures hipsters with Northern Thai cooking that isn't handcuffed to please the lowest common denominator, as well as wine pairings that perfectly complement the bold flavors. Classic minced chicken laap is ratcheted up, while the crispy fried tofu's Thai chili-enhanced sauce knocks out with a one-two punch.

▮ 1511 17th St. NW (bet. P & Q Sts.)
▣ Dupont Circle
✆ N/A — **WEB:** www.littleserow.com
▮ Dinner Tue – Sat   PRICE: $$

LUPO VERDE ꭑꝋ

Italian • *Rustic*

MAP: 2-B4

The neighborhood is hopping with a crowded, convivial vibe and Lupo Verde dances to that same beat. This two-storied restaurant has an osteria feel to its downstairs level, where a Carrara marble bar and communal wood tables welcome diners. Upstairs, the dining room has a low-key but quintessential luxe Italian look.

The kitchen too boasts some unique offerings—a roasted onion stuffed with four-cheese fondue is delicious, but it's really all about the homemade pasta and spot-on affetati here. The spaghetti is gloriously thick and chewy, while the charcuterie boards are crammed with delicious imported salumi, cheeses, olives and giardiniera. Finish with a classic affogato, in which a shot of hot espresso is poured over a dollop of creamy vanilla ice cream.

▮ 1401 T St. NW (at 14th St.)
▣ U St
✆ (202) 827-4752 — **WEB:** www.lupoverdedc.com
▮ Lunch Sat – Sun Dinner nightly   PRICE: $$

MAKETTO

Asian • Contemporary décor

MAP: 8-C4

Maketto is the love child of the hip gods of fashion and food. Walk in off ever-changing H Street and you'll instantly be met with glittering cases brimming with eyewear and accessories. Stave off the urge to shop (for now) and focus on the menu instead—a mod mashup of Cambodian and Taiwanese items. Coupled with inventive cocktails, it is proof positive that this is far from your average department store diner.

Braised pork bao is a sumptuous handheld treat by day and appears platter-style at night. Crispy chicken wings with pickled chili peppers are the perfect bar snack, while duck noodle soup is über-flavorful with just a bit of sweet. Speaking of which, pastries are available all day—and those long Chinese donuts taste like churros, only better.

1351 H St. NE (bet. Linden Ct. & 14th St.)
(202) 838-9972 — **WEB:** www.maketto1351.com
Lunch daily Dinner Mon – Sat **PRICE:** $$

MAKOTO

Japanese • Minimalist

MAP: 7-B1

Makoto is a testament to the love between a father and son. The chef, who assumed the top spot when his father passed some years ago, is warm and generous with stories of his father's passion and sacrifice. This place isn't about trends and there is a palpable sense of honoring tradition, so make a reservation, dress up and expect to shed your shoes at the door.

You won't find à la carte sushi here, but you will be rewarded with a litany of skillfully prepared dishes. Seared Turkish royal sea bass with grilled asparagus and sugar snap peas along with a roasted red pepper sauce displays harmonious balance. Then pan-seared sea urchin with crispy rice cake, burnt nori and kinome leaf, sprinkled with green seaweed, is named a signature for good reason.

4822 MacArthur Blvd. NW (bet. Reservoir Rd. & W St.)
(202) 298-6866 — **WEB:** www.makotorestaurantdc.com
Dinner Tue – Thu **PRICE:** $$$

MANDU

Korean • Simple

MAP: 2-A4

You don't come to Mandu with your high-maintenance friend. But, if you're seeking the real deal—authentic and delicious Korean food without a lot of fuss—it is just the place. Everything is made with love at this family-owned original, and the portions are generous (especially at brunch, which is also light on the wallet).

Stick to the stews—dak jjim or soon doobu, yokge jang and mandu guk—before moving up to the more hearty galbi or bulgogi. Kimchi jjigae has a heady perfume of garlic, chilies and onions that announces its presence right after leaving the semi-open kitchen. And the kimchi bokumbap, heaped into a deep stone bowl, has a sweet-spicy sauce and is flavored with just the right amount of gochujang to add color and extra oomph.

■ 1805 18th St. NW (bet. S & Swann Sts.)
🚇 Dupont Circle
✆ (202) 588-1540 — **WEB:** www.mandudc.com
■ Lunch & dinner daily

PRICE: $$

MARCEL'S

French • Elegant

MAP: 1-A3

Marcel's may lure a who's who crowd to its elegantly understated dining room, but there's nothing uppity about the amiable and genuine staff, who expertly walk the tightrope between attentive and fussy. Patrons come to linger over French-influenced meals enjoyed over multiple courses.

Pan-seared foie gras atop duck confit and paired with eau de vie-soaked cherries, or grilled quail over a warm artichoke salad are certainly French inspired. Curried butternut squash soup with apple, black sesame and toasted cashew or enoki mushroom-topped halibut over parsnip purée speak to an entirely different influence. The almond financier with sunflower ice cream might be overdressed with too many flourishes, but with its buttery goodness, nobody is complaining.

■ 2401 Pennsylvania Ave. NW (bet. 24th & 25th Sts.)
🚇 Foggy Bottom-GWU
✆ (202) 296-1166 — **WEB:** www.marcelsdc.com
■ Dinner nightly

PRICE: $$$$

MASSERIA

Italian • Contemporary décor

MAP: 8-A2

With its chic and seamless blend of indoor and outdoor space, Masseria is a clear departure from its simpler surrounds. The classic former warehouse—complete with the requisite exposed ducts, concrete floors and brick walls—has been glammed up with a stainless steel exhibition kitchen, chrome and leather furnishings, pendant lights suspended from nautical rope and an impressive glass-encased wine cellar.

It's all very relaxed, albeit in a well-dressed way, and the feel-good vibe extends to the staff, who clearly like working here as much as diners enjoy lingering over the multi-course meals.

Chef/owner Nicholas Stefanelli's Puglian heritage comes through in the menu, which features three to five courses, along with a nightly tasting. The kitchen hits all the right notes balancing trendy and serious. Begin with a cigar box filled with focaccia so sinfully delicious, you'll be tempted to scarf it all down—but don't. You'll want to save room for the spicy fish stew, a thing of beauty practically brimming with tripe and lobster, or house-made maccheroni with a thick and gamey goat ragù. Even dessert strays far from the pack, showcasing beet ice cream instead of the classic tiramisu.

■ 1340 4th St. NE (bet. Neal Pl. & Penn St.)

▥ NoMa-Gallaudet U

℘ (202) 608-1330 — **WEB:** www.masseria-dc.com

■ Dinner Tue – Sat

PRICE: $$$

MAYDĀN

Middle Eastern • Rustic

MAP: 2-B3

Travel down a charming alleyway in search of a blue door, as it's the only sign you've arrived (the line, which begins forming at 4:30 P.M., is another hint). Once inside you'll feel you've been spirited away to a bedouin's haven.

Maydān's soul is the first-floor's open-fire hearth, where pit masters choreograph a dizzying ballet of meat-centric activity. This menu is a love letter to the culinary traditions of Beirut, Batumi, Tangier and Tehran and includes smoky halloumi, fire-roasted eggplant and Beiruti hummus. While some savor the bitter tenderness of dandelion greens, others revel in the sweet deliciousness from saffron-spiced beef skewers or lamb kebabs with ground pistachios. Of course, that slow-cooked duck breast is positively drool-worthy.

- 1346 Florida Ave. NW (bet. 13th & 14th Sts.)
- U St.
- (202) 370-3696 — **WEB:** www.maydandc.com
- Dinner nightly

PRICE: $$

MILLIE'S

Seafood • Family

MAP: N/A

Take a break from the Beltway and head to Millie's. It's an offshoot of the Nantucket original, with a loyal whale-patterned, shorts-wearing crowd. Sound preppy? It is. The space nails that breezy, nautical vibe with navy blue booths, a ceiling strung with boats and not-too-twee ship lanterns. It's almost impossible not to be cheerful here—even the open kitchen buzzes with activity, simply enhancing the convivial aura.

Equally upbeat is the menu that shines a spotlight on New England. Seared tuna tacos with wasabi cream and ceviche are light and refreshing; while the heady fragrance of the blue crab fried rice will induce envy from nearby tables. Maryland crab cake piled atop a fluffy brioche and slathered with herb aïoli tastes of summer by the sea.

- 4866 Massachusetts Ave. NW (bet. Fordham Rd. & 48th St.)
- (202) 733-5789 — **WEB:** www.milliesdc.com
- Lunch & dinner daily

PRICE: $$

MÉTIER ✿

Contemporary · Elegant

MAP: 3-B2

Find this mature, splurge-worthy tasting room beneath its smartly decked out sibling, Kinship. They may share a kitchen and chef/owner, but these are two distinct restaurants.

Guests enter Métier via an elevator, which then leads to a second, more sultry lounge. With a fireplace and shelves lined with cookbooks, this is a lovely stop for cocktails and nibbles. One part living room and two parts art gallery, the sleek arena is a spare collection of cloth-robed tables and white walls with paintings here and there. This is one of those few remaining places where jackets are required, so gentlemen, don't forget to don them!

The name, Métier, is defined as an area of expertise, and that proves true in an ambitious menu reflective of Chef Eric Ziebold's experience. The bright, tart and oh-so-French spring garlic bavarois and the asparagus fricassee are signs of the season, while the Great Lakes walleye pike over pine nut butter, frisée, turnips and cured rhubarb shines with subtlety. The potato-crusted veal sweetbreads over corned beef short ribs and pickled celtuce brunoise sport a delightful tartness. Cumin-spiced lamb leans Middle Eastern, while key lime meringue is decidedly American.

▢ 1015 7th St. NW (bet. L St. & New York Ave.)

▣ Mt Vernon Sq

✆ (202) 737-7500 — **WEB:** www.metierdc.com

▢ Dinner Wed – Sat

PRICE: $$$$

MINIBAR ✿✿

Contemporary • Design

MAP: 3-B3

Two frosted doors mark the entrance to minibar—a restaurant that extends well beyond its diminutive name. The stylish entry lounge is an idyllic stop for a glass of bubbly before heading into the dimly lit laboratory-like dining room. Here, guests are situated at six seats per dining counter, all set around Chef José Andrés' stainless steel workspace that literally makes his world a stage.

The lab-like décor isn't a coincidence, since the modern cooking on display here is highly experimental (though deftly avoids mad scientist status). The kitchen takes familiar tastes and ingredients and cheekily transforms them into something new and unexpected. There are those famous liquid olives, of course, as well as meaty morels served with "peas" that are actually "pearls" filled with fragrant pea and mint. Playful course after course remind one that a snail is not just a snail here, but a dome of Ibérico ham gel, formed like that mollusk, served with rabbit jus and escargot roe. A ring of fried Krispy Kreme donut ice cream is appropriately tongue-in-cheek, but the whimsy never comes at the expense of wit. Despite the sense of humor, this kitchen's serious effort should never be taken lightly.

■ 855 E St. NW (at 9th St.)

🚇 Gallery Pl-Chinatown

✆ (202) 393-0812 — **WEB:** www.minibarbyjoseandres.com

■ Dinner Tue – Sat   **PRICE:** $$$$

MINTWOOD PLACE

American • Neighborhood

WASHINGTON

MAP: 2-A3

Take a chic Parisian and a ten gallon-hat-wearing cowboy and blend for an improbable but oh-so-happy mix and you have Mintwood Place. This Western saloon-style space does Adams Morgan proud with its fun-loving, quirky feel defined by wood paneling, wrought-iron accents and a rooster- and wagon wheel-enhanced décor.

Don't worry though, as this melting pot of American and French cooking is anything but hokey. Snack on deviled eggs and pickled rhubarb before digging into escargot hushpuppies, a glorious Franco-American meeting of the minds. Starters like goat cheese and beet mountain pie or duck pâté entice with French finesse, while entrées like shrimp and grits or smoked pork ribs are stick-to-your-ribs, Southern-style good. Key lime pie is perfection.

■ 1813 Colombia Rd. NW (bet. Biltmore St. & Mintwood Pl.)

℗ (202) 234-6732 — **WEB:** www.mintwoodplace.com

■ Lunch Sat – Sun Dinner Tue – Sun   PRICE: $$$

MIRABELLE

French • Luxury

MAP: 1-C3

From its walnut-framed tufted leather walls and Carrara marble floors to the smoky mirrors and captivating double-spouted absinthe fountain, this no-expense-spared stunner just blocks from the White House does wonders for French-American relations. And thanks to heavy-hitters Frank Ruta and Aggie Chin, the classic brasserie food is as polished as the scene.

Sip a cocktail or glass of wine from the well-chosen list before diving in to crowd-pleasing dishes such as oven-roasted poussin, enhanced with a deliciously rich crayfish-mushroom cream sauce. Beef tartare, in all of its glistening ruby glory, is textbook perfect. Then there's dessert—mais oui! Tarte Tatin, yuzu sesame mille crêpe or butterscotch crémeux practically deserve to be eaten first.

■ 900 16th St. NW (at I St.)

🚇 Farragut West

℗ (202) 506-3833 — **WEB:** www.mirabelledc.com

■ Lunch Mon – Fri Dinner Mon – Sat   PRICE: $$$

MOLA 🐸

Spanish • Contemporary décor

MAP: 2-B2

Sequestered into the second floor of a townhouse, light-washed walls, blonde wood furnishings, subdued art and sprays of poppies lend an ethereal, calm energy to this Spanish tapas gem.

The menu kicks things up a notch, layering bright and bold flavors throughout their items. Small plate starters might reveal tender white asparagus laced with pea shoot "pesto," aioli and deliciously salty Serrano; or tender little ham croquetas, served with sharp mojo verde and folded with creamy béchamel. Seafood and meat options also abound, all well executed, but some notable vegetable preparations steal the show. For instance, pan-fried mushrooms on toast are punched up with manchego; while olive oil- and sherry-braised artichokes are coupled with a pine nut sauce.

3155 Mt. Pleasant St. NW (bet. Kenyon St. & Kilbourne Pl.)
Columbia Heights
(202) 849-3247 — **WEB:** www.moladc.com
Dinner nightly   PRICE: $$

MOMOFUKU CCDC 🍴

Asian • Trendy

♿ 📷   **MAP:** 3-A2

David Chang has come a long way since his tiny game-changing original in New York City's East Village. This impressive DC outpost is bright and shiny with multiple levels, lots of glass and textbook-contemporary décor (think backless blonde wood stools).

Executive Chef Tae Strain carries on Chang's signature street-style food that put him on the map, and that's exactly what you'll find here. Those buzzed-about buns (let's face it, that's what you came for) are the stuff that pilgrimages are made of: pillowy soft, stuffed with meat or shrimp and slathered with tangy sauces. Rice cakes are yet another favored dish, while braised fried chicken is oh-so-good. Located just off the main dining room, the takeout Milk Bar carries desserts like the famed crack pie.

1090 I St. NW (at New York Ave.)
McPherson Square
(202) 602-1832 — **WEB:** www.momofuku.com/ccdc
Lunch & dinner daily   PRICE: $$

NAPOLI PASTA BAR

Italian • Trattoria

MAP: 2-C2

Luciano De Crescenzo wrote dreamily about "gatto' di patate" in Frijenno Magnanno, his anthology of Neapolitan dishes, and indeed, the potato cake at this «pasta bar» is bang on. Throw in a sweet little location on burgeoning Sherman Avenue, and it's hard not to love this neighborhood spot.

Begin your meal with the aforementioned regional dish, featuring a béchamel sauce blended with potatoes and cubes of pancetta. Then move on to more gorgeous items, like the paccheri 'o rrau—toothsome tube-shaped pasta laced with a sumptuous tomato ragù that is crowned by parmesan and basil. For a heartier dinner, try your hand at the pollo del faito, a pair of tender chicken breasts topped with cherry tomatoes, pancetta and spicy chili pepper flakes.

- 2737 Sherman Ave. NW (at Girard St.)
- U St
- (202) 588-8752 — **WEB:** www.napolipastabar.com
- Dinner Tue – Sun   PRICE: $$

NAZCA MOCHICA

Peruvian • Contemporary décor

MAP: 1-C1

In a Peruvian version of upstairs-downstairs, this two-in-one restaurant comprises a cebiche and pisco bar downstairs with more traditional dining and a sleeker style upstairs. Luckily, the fantastic cebiches are served both up and down. Causitas are the ultimate spud lover's comfort food and feature four towers of baked whipped potatoes topped with different flavors: caramelized fatty pork belly and onions; chicken salad dressed in mild aji amarillo; tuna cebiche with cilantro shoots; and slivered roasted piquillo peppers.

Kobe short ribs are glazed with a terrific, mildly spicy aji panca-honey, accompanied by yuca, potatoes and choclo in a creamy huancaina sauce. Sugar-dusted alfajores filled with dulce de leche at the end round out the meal.

- 1633 P St. NW (bet. 17th & 16th Sts.)
- Dupont Circle
- (202) 733-3170 — **WEB:** www.nazcamochica.com
- Lunch daily Dinner Tue – Sun   PRICE: $$

NOPA KITCHEN + BAR

American • *Contemporary décor*

MAP: 3-B3

Don't let its location next to the popular Spy Museum in Penn Quarters throw you off: there's serious food to be had at NoPa Kitchen + Bar, and the locals rubbing elbows with the tourists prove it. Opened in 2013 by the talented restaurant group behind Rasika and The Oval Room, this sibling is named for its location north of Pennsylvania Avenue.

Enter up a set of stairs to land at a welcoming bar, or head to the right and choose a seat in one of the two modern dining spaces, fitted out in exposed brick, shiny hardware and a few private nooks for larger parties. Dinner might begin with excellent curried chicken meatballs; and then progress to an irresistible torchietti pasta laced with lamb bolognese, tender green chickpeas and savory 'nduja breadcrumbs.

- 800 F St. NW (at 8th St.)
- Gallery Pl-Chinatown
- (202) 347-4667 — **WEB:** www.nopadc.com
- Lunch & dinner daily

PRICE: $$

OBELISK

Italian • *Cozy*

MAP: 1-B1

Obelisk attracts a surprisingly young, casual crowd for a spot that has been serving a fixed five-course menu five nights a week since 1987. This is a fact that's likely due to the restaurant's warm, neighborhood feel, even if the townhome it's set in could use a revamp.

The light and seasonal Italian cooking begins with a bang as an assortment of fantastic antipasti is quickly ushered to the table: creamy burrata; a sardine served over a tasty Prosecco-braised onion salad; crunchy puntarelle salad with a creamy anchovy dressing; and a thin slice of porchetta with a crisp shell and rich, flavorful meaty center, to name a few. The second and third courses are overshadowed by the first, but the full experience is worth the two to three hours to enjoy.

- 2029 P St. NW (bet. 20th & 21st Sts.)
- Dupont Circle
- (202) 872-1180 — **WEB:** www.obeliskdc.com
- Dinner Tue – Sat

PRICE: $$$

OSTERIA MORINI 🍴⃝

Italian • Contemporary décor

♿ ⛺ 🛋️

MAP: 4-A4

Yards Park is shaking things up along the Anacostia River, and Osteria Morini is among the high-profile restaurants headlining the riverfront rags-to-riches development. Thanks to its giant windows, abundant natural light and open kitchen, this sleek and airy space truly shines.

One of several spinoffs of Chef Michael White's original in New York's SoHo, the menu manages to be both impressive and familiar. Get the much-touted burger, which is composed of the chef's own special meat blend, and hugely celebrated at lunch. Other items may include wood-grilled meats, homemade pasta and polpettine in brodo. Most impressive, however, is the generous bowl of conchiglie topped with pecorino fonduta, a culinary delight that screams "dig in" like nothing else.

▪ 301 Water St. SE (bet. 3rd & 4th Sts.)
🚇 Navy Yard-Ballpark
✆ (202) 484-0660 — **WEB:** www.osteriamorini.com
▪ Lunch & dinner daily   PRICE: $$$

OTTOMAN TAVERNA 😀

Turkish • Contemporary décor

🍺 ♿ ⛺ 📺 🛋️

MAP: 3-C2

This place is fit for a king. The interior is drop-dead gorgeous with a can't-stop-staring décor. From its honeycomb patterns on the walls and that large mural of the Hagia Sophia, to its whitewashed walls with glimmering deep-blue pendants, this restaurant brings a little bit of Istanbul to the Mt. Vernon Triangle.

Sip a cool apple-rose tea while perusing the menu of Turkish cuisine infused with a modern bent. Kirmizi mercimek corbasi is a refreshing red lentil soup that starts things off right. Then dive in to thinly sliced and delicious lamb and beef kebabs. But it's the moussaka, with its supple eggplant, potato slices and cinnamon-scented lamb, that must not be skipped. Freshly baked baklava or Noah's pudding end the meal on a syrupy note.

▪ 425 I St. NW (bet. 4th & 5th Sts.)
🚇 Gallery Pl-Chinatown
✆ (202) 847-0395 — **WEB:** www.ottomantaverna.com
▪ Lunch & dinner daily   PRICE: $$

THE OVAL ROOM

Contemporary · Elegant

MAP: 1-C4

The Oval Room has been the restaurant of choice for a particular brand of Beltway insiders for over two decades, but like any doyenne worth her salt, this Knightsbridge Restaurant Group gem strives to keep everything fresh. The dining room oozes sophistication with its plush carpeting and museum-style artwork. This elegance also extends outdoors to the chic sidewalk.

The food echoes the sophisticated environs with well-prepared classics, such as chicken liver mousse and crisp-skinned Amish roast chicken with Brussels sprouts, wild mushrooms, sweet peas and shaved truffle. Other entrées, such as shrimp and coconut grits with shellfish butter, or even molasses-glazed pork belly with cornbread purée show off a creative and Southern-inspired flair.

- 800 Connecticut Ave. NW (bet. 16th & 17th Sts.)
- Farragut West
- (202) 463-8700 — **WEB:** www.ovalroom.com
- Lunch Mon – Fri Dinner Mon – Sat

PRICE: $$$

OYAMEL

Mexican · Contemporary décor

MAP: 3-B4

Patience is a virtue at this fun, festive and ultra-popular Mexican destination. Can they help it if they're packed most nights? Chef José Andrés knows his food and the loyal crowds here bear testament. Snag a seat at the entertaining ceviche bar and guzzle thirst-quenching drinks while snacking on small plates.

The kitchen's dedication to technique and ingredients is clear, with a particular penchant for south-of-the-border cuisine like huevos enfrijoladas, crispy chilaquiles and gorditas topped with Hudson Valley duck confit. Don't miss the tarasca estilo pátzcuaro though, an otherworldly black bean soup with avocado leaves, swirls of crema and crumbled cotija. The lunch special, which the menu refers to as "Almuerzo Rápido," is a steal at $20.

- 401 7th St. NW (bet. D & E Sts.)
- Archives
- (202) 628-1005 — **WEB:** www.oyamel.com
- Lunch & dinner daily

PRICE: $$

PANDA GOURMET

Chinese • *Simple*

MAP: 8-C1

The name may look familiar, but don't confuse this gem with the ubiquitous food court spot. Sure, Panda Gourmet isn't winning any awards for its lackluster locale set amidst gas stations and fast-food chains, but you're here for the food, not frills. And that food, well, it's quality Sichuan and Shaanxi cuisine brought to you at great value.

The heat is turned down for more sensitive palates, but there's plenty of flavor packed into these dishes. Hangzhou beef soup could feed an army with its soothing and satisfying broth, cubes of firm tofu, beef and loads of cilantro. Then rice noodles with minced pork is kicked up a notch with fiery chili oil, and may be tailed by mapo tofu, sprinkled with ground pork, green onions and spicy red chili sauce.

2700 New York Ave. NE (at Bladensburg Rd.)
(202) 534-1620 — **WEB:** N/A
Lunch & dinner daily

PRICE: $$

THE PARTISAN

Gastropub • *Rustic*

MAP: 3-B4

It shares space with sib Red Apron, a butcher shop and gourmet boutique, but The Partisan wins votes for its gastropub grub and hip vibe. It's tall, dark and handsome: picture industrial-height ceilings with exposed air ducts and a moody-broody color scheme.

Beer is big here, with more than 20 on draft and arranged by flavor profile (tart/funky and fruit/spice are just two). At lunch, pick a meat (turkey breast, porchetta or beef döner), then take your tigelle or flatbread and smoosh it all together. At night, the menu steers offbeat and may include crawfish hushpuppies, beer-brined rotisserie duck or smoked pork with mescal-baked beans. Charcuterie is also creative, unveiling absinthe-lime rillettes and negroni-inspired Campari-rosemary salami.

709 D St. NW (bet. 7th & 8th Sts.)
Archives
(202) 524-5322 — **WEB:** www.thepartisandc.com
Lunch & dinner daily

PRICE: $$

PEARL DIVE OYSTER PALACE

Southern • *Tavern*

MAP: 1-D1

With its slightly nautical ambience and casual pub vibe, this spot makes an ideal clubhouse for play-hard types. And while places that look this good usually don't have the menu to match, Pearl Dive's kitchen gives the dining room a run for its money.

The lineup is true-blue American food with a Southern slant, spotlighting starters like crunchy crawfish fritters, regional gumbos and entrées like Tchoupitoulas—oyster confit with blue crab, Tasso ham as well as roasted corn. And then there are the incredible oysters, which are part of the Oyster Recovery Project (meaning you can feel good while you slurp them up with abandon). On your way out, make like the smug, in-the-know patrons and order the Brazos River-bottom pecan pie to go.

- 1612 14th St. NW (bet. Q & Corcoran Sts.)
- U St
- (202) 319-1612 — **WEB:** www.pearldivedc.com
- Lunch Fri – Sun Dinner nightly   **PRICE:** $$

PROOF

American • *Contemporary décor*

MAP: 3-B3

It may be said that the proof is in the pudding, but this particular restaurant proves its mettle with wine. Inside, contemporary pendant lights, dark wood floors and walls showcasing bottles of, yes, wine, have a chic and modern effect. The liquid is more than artwork, though, and oenophiles and newbies alike will find satisfying sips.

Proof's food reflects an international point of view—envision flaky and glistening flatbread topped with chickpeas, red onion, green olives, pickled radish and a silky, smoked eggplant emulsion; or spicy chicken and pork meatballs paired with ricotta ravioli. If you manage to leave room for dessert, consider forgoing something sweet and instead sink your teeth into a selection from the comprehensive cheese list.

- 775 G St. NW (at 8th St.)
- Gallery Pl-Chinatown
- (202) 737-7663 — **WEB:** www.proofdc.com
- Lunch Tue – Fri & Sunday Dinner nightly   **PRICE:** $$

PINEAPPLE AND PEARLS ✿✿

Contemporary • Intimate

What makes this "pearl" such a memorable dining experience is that the cooking is ambitious yet whimsical, and completely devoid of formality or fuss. Whether the bartender or Chef de Cuisine Scott Muns serves you, no one in this kitchen seems self-important. Your continued enjoyment is paramount—an honorable feat considering that you're in for a meal that occupies most of your night. This small space may be packed, but the ambience is pleasant and very comfortable. Know that the prix-fixe includes beverage pairings, but guests seated at the bar may choose to order drinks à la carte instead. No matter where you land, dishes spark interest and service remains at its highest level.

Roasted turbot carved tableside is set over mustard cream that melts in your mouth. Filled with Robiola Bosina and smoked dates as well as charred potatoes and nettles, raviolo doppio presents a terrific flavor combination. Tradition is also clearly revered here by way of veal sweetbreads en croute, a savory pastry layered with mushroom duxelles, chicken boudin and, of course, sweetbreads, for a richly satisfying twist.

Desserts never fail to surprise, as seen in the wonderful carrot cake with parsley gelato.

■ 715 8th St. SE (bet. G & I Sts.)

🚇 Eastern Market

𝒫 (202) 595-7375 — **WEB:** www.pineappleandpearls.com

■ Dinner Tue – Fri   **PRICE: $$$$**

PLUME

European · Luxury

There is hardly a more civilized dining experience than the one offered at Plume, where you can rest assured of some seriously well-dressed and good-looking company.

Tucked inside the stately Jefferson Hotel, where signed documents by President Thomas Jefferson double as design elements, this dining room echoes that mood without ever feeling fusty or musty. Dinner is a well-orchestrated symphony that may commence with an amuse-bouche of chive custard, flecked with crabmeat and artistically presented in a mini jar. This is a sure sign of other, more creative things to come—including a seasonal spectacle of parsnip and Comté ravioli in a charred leek soubise. Then New Zealand venison served with lingonberry sauce is so good you may even want to take a swipe at sopping up every last drop, while an almond-and-orange confection coupled with a rich chocolate mousse and spiced wine sorbet makes for an exalted finale.

The wine list spotlights the world's top regions, but diners should ask the sommelier about top bottlings from Virginia's best producers. The late president's Lafitte may have been a fake, but the Madeira selection is par excellence with vintages that date all the way back to 1720.

■ 1200 16th St. NW (at M St.)

▥ Farragut North

☏ (202) 448-2300 — **WEB:** www.plumedc.com

■ Dinner Tue – Sat   PRICE: **$$$$**

PURPLE PATCH
Filipino • Neighborhood

                          MAP: 2-B2

How do you pay tribute to the classics while simultaneously bumping them up ever so much? Just ask the Purple Patch. This restaurant delivers note-perfect Filipino food with just the right amount of playfulness. Case in point? The adobo-radicchio wraps, which take the familiar flavors of chicken in adobo, top it with pickled papaya, then surround it with the crunch of radicchio. Pork sinigang is considered a typical (read staple) dish, but is truly worthy of exaltation. Here, tender chunks of pork are bathed in a lemon broth that is so generously sized it seems indecent, and with potatoes, vegetables and fluffy jasmine rice, it's plain sinful.

Even dessert is a thing of wonder. Purple yam ice cream? Who knew a tuber could be this magically delicious?

▪ 3155 Mt. Pleasant St. NW (bet. Keyton St. & Kilbourne Pl.)
▪ Columbia Heights
℘ (202) 299-0022 — **WEB:** www.purplepatchdc.com
▪ Lunch Sat – Sun Dinner nightly   PRICE: ⌖

RAPPAHANNOCK OYSTER BAR
Seafood • Simple

🍸 ♿ 🏠   **MAP:** 8-A2

Set inside the buzzing Union Market, Rappahannock Oyster Bar is so much more than a popular bivalve joint. The feel-good revival story behind it will make you feel more philanthropist than hungry diner, and the ambience is everything you'd expect and then some: counter space, communal seating, a sprinkling of outdoor tables and an open-air vibe.

While the spotlight here is on the raw bar (order the sampler, a veritable love letter to the Virginia waters), the cooked dishes give those half-shells a run for their money. Clam chowder is thick, creamy and full of briny meat; and though the steamed shrimp dish sounds simple, these spicy shell-on specimens, served with a hunk of bread, sautéed onions and peppers are a messy but delicious affair.

▪ 1309 5th St. NE (in Union Market)
▪ NoMa-Gallaudet U
℘ (202) 544-4702 — **WEB:** www.rroysters.com
▪ Lunch & dinner Tue – Sun   PRICE: $$

RASIKA

Indian • *Contemporary décor*

MAP: 3-B4

With easy access to the metro, this is a good-looking, loud and lively spot that lures all types of diners. Everyone is here for their kitsch-free Indian cuisine and laid-back ambience—both of which are as perfectly suited for a casual night out with friends as they are for a formal dinner with colleagues or festive celebration.

It's difficult to live up to the hype, but Rasika turns out several winning dishes. Grab a seat at the back counter for views into the kitchen, which turns out such highlights as crispy palak chaat tossed with raita, tamarind and date chutneys. Then crunchy okra displays a perfect blend of spicy and sour flavors. Match this with top house-made cubes of paneer, skewered with peppers, onions and accompanied by a tangy green sauce.

 633 D St. NW (bet. 6th & 7th Sts.)

📞 (202) 637-1222 — **WEB:** www.rasikarestaurant.com

Lunch Mon – Fri Dinner Mon – Sat   **PRICE:** $$$

THE RED HEN 😊

Italian • *Neighborhood*

MAP: 2-D4

You'll want to wake up with the rooster to score a reservation at this rustic Italian gem as it's incredibly popular, and ergo, always packed. Walk-ins can snag a seat at the three-sided bar that anchors the room, decked out in full country charm with exposed brick walls, reclaimed timber and beamed ceilings. What's so special, you ask? The food, of course, which is terrific. Pastas are spot on and include cacio e pepe "arancini," crowd-favorite mezzi rigatoni or even the mafalde verde—a sweet-and-savory combo of braised duck ragù, Calabrian chili and pecorino romano. Entrées like grilled short rib or scallops with pickled chili aïoli are also exquisite.

The short wine list features unusual selections (Slovenia, anyone?) and very affordable prices.

1822 1st St. NW (at Seaton Pl.)

📞 (202) 525-3021 — **WEB:** www.theredhendc.com

Dinner nightly   **PRICE:** $$

RIS

American • *Contemporary décor*

MAP: 1-A3

Ris Lacoste helms the stove at this terrific neighborhood spot, a draw for diners in the company of family, business associates and lovers alike. The sprawling, light-filled dining room is dressed in earth tones and filled with intimate corners for an air of seductive sophistication. And the menu, with its ramped-up takes on the tried-and-true, toes the line between familiar and surprising.

Loaded with butter and olive oil and jazzed up with red pepper flakes, linguine with clams is briny and delicious and chicken Milanese has just the right amount of breading beneath its zippy tomato topping. Even the crown of cauliflower is interesting and complex, thanks to an ensemble of roasted vegetables slicked with mustard cream and an army of flavors.

- 2275 L St. NW (at 23rd St.)
- Foggy Bottom-GWU
- (202) 730-2500 — **WEB:** www.risdc.com
- Lunch Sun – Fri Dinner nightly

PRICE: $$

ROYAL

Latin American • *Neighborhood*

MAP: 2-D4

This airy, lovely and welcoming neighborhood respite likes to keep things low-maintenance. There's no host or reservations accepted here, but the price point is agreeably lower than its fussier neighbors. The family that owns the restaurant has a solid hand in this all-day operation (don't miss breakfast), and it's designed to offer scrumptious food without breaking the bank.

At dinnertime, head to the intimate second-level dining space—done up in original details like tin ceilings—and try your hand at dishes like tender pork empanadas, laced with aji and the heavenly scent of garlic. The masa "gnocchi" is a real treat, with its knobs of dough tossed with braised beef, maitake mushrooms, cotija cheese, crispy crumbs and loads of herbs.

- 501 Florida Ave. NW (at 5th St.)
- Shaw-Howard U
- (202) 332-7777 — **WEB:** www.theroyaldc.com
- Lunch & dinner daily

PRICE: $$

ROSE'S LUXURY

Contemporary · *Trendy*

MAP: 4-C2

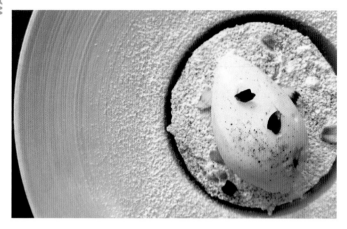

To dine now or later, that is the question. Enter Rose's Luxury and you'll need to decide whether you're heading upstairs for drinks or settling right in for a meal at one of their four nooks.

This space exudes fun, especially at the counter facing the busy kitchen. The décor is decidedly laidback, highlighting bare wood tables and exposed bulbs that can make you feel like you're in someone's backyard. This casual mood means you'll spot all types inside, including couples with tots in tow. The kitchen does its greatest work at the beginning and end, though there are many family-style dishes on offer. Small plates, such as the ricotta served with grilled brioche and an intensely flavorful lychee salad with pork sausage, are pitch perfect. Desserts are similarly stirring and indeed a good reason to save room here. In fact, some may even skip dinner for the often befuddling, intriguing and just plain delicious take on the classics. Sweet, poached, and almost candied cubes of eggplant turn the familiar tarte Tatin on its head, just as the Fernet-Cola tiramisu is notably unusual yet blindingly good.

Those on the run may load up on breakfast and lunch at precious Little Pearl nearby.

■ 717 8th St. SE (bet. G & I Sts.)

▦ Eastern Market

℘ (202) 580-8889 — **WEB:** www.rosesluxury.com

■ Dinner Mon – Sat

PRICE: $$

SABABA
Mediterranean · Chic

MAP: 5-C1

"Sababa," which means "cool" in Hebrew slang, is exactly as advertised. Sharing a wall and connected by a gorgeous zinc bar to Bindaas next door, this Mid-East ode is awash in Mediterranean tiles. But despite the hip digs, it's all about food here.

The fine-tuned menu features Israeli salads, dips and kebabs, but small plates are its heart and soul. Start with salatim, a five-salad starter. Then choose from dishes such as charred eggplant with herbed labneh, fried cauliflower with tahini and raisins or pomegranate-glazed chicken liver. The list goes on, but one thing to never skip is the hummus. It's so much more than the usual, that it's even listed as a daily special. Keeping in line with the sauce is their Israeli- and Greek-focused wine list.

- 3311 Connecticut Ave NW (at Macomb St.)
- Cleveland Park
- (202) 244-6750 — **WEB:** www.sababauptown.com
- Lunch Sat – Sun Dinner nightly   PRICE: $$

SAKURAMEN ⓘⓞ
Japanese · Simple

MAP: 2-A3

Sometimes all you really want is a delicious meal in a comfortable setting. No fuss, no hipper-than-thou patrons, just good food. Sakuramen, in the basement of a row house in Adams Morgan, is on hand to soothe your soul with its wide variety of that steaming bowl of love—ramen.

In fact, it's all about these toothsome noodles here. Goji ramen is a traditional shoyu ramen, while chosun shows off a Korean influence with Angus bulgogi and kimchi. Gyoza and steamed buns are available for good measure. Sakuramen is naturally the house special and the kitchen changes things up with a vegetable broth made from mushrooms and seaweed. Braised bamboo shoots, portobello caps and other vegetables bob amid the curly noodles for a perfectly satisfying meal.

- 2441 18th St. NW (bet. Belmont & Columbia Rds.)
- (202) 656-5285 — **WEB:** www.sakuramen.info
- Lunch Fri – Sun Dinner Tue – Sun   PRICE: ⓔⓢ

SALLY'S MIDDLE NAME

American • *Neighborhood*

MAP: 8-C4

Delicious, uncomplicated food is the name of the game here at this three-name and tri-level restaurant with a popular rooftop. Inside, the décor echoes the kitchen's "keep it simple" mantra, with little more to look at than unadorned white tiles and a pile of gently worn cookbooks in the corner.

There are just over two-dozen selections on this daily changing menu, where vegetables make a big impression. Expect dishes to come as promised: green tomatoes are indeed that, diced perfectly then ramped up slightly with a smoky minced-bacon vinaigrette. Fried clams are set atop a house-made tartar sauce and smack of a summer day at the beach, while the "new bay" chicken thigh punches up the classic Old Bay seasoning with curry for a bit more kick.

■ 1320 H St. NE (bet. 13th & 14th Sts.)
✆ (202) 750-6529 — **WEB:** www.sallysmiddlename.com
■ Lunch Sat – Sun Dinner Wed – Sun   **PRICE: $$**

1789

American • *Historic*

MAP: 6-A2

Housed on a quaint street, 1789 is classic Georgetown—think wooden beams, antiques and fireplaces all nestled inside a historic, Federal period townhouse. The restaurant's six dining rooms, each with their own layout and décor, are spread across three floors and packed with a global, multi-generational crowd.

The mood is definitely special occasion, and the menu bows to that by sticking with what works: straightforward, seasonal and carefully curated American fare. Maryland crab fondue set over silky mashed potatoes and topped with uni is winningly simple; while wonderfully moist duck breast is dressed up with a foie gras truffle for a luxe garnish. Coconut milk cream with passion fruit crèmeux is that ideal yin and yang of sweet and tart.

■ 1226 36th St. NW (at Prospect St.)
✆ (202) 965-1789 — **WEB:** www.1789restaurant.com
■ Dinner nightly   **PRICE: $$$$**

SFOGLINA

Italian • Chic

MAP: 5-B1

This focused, consistent and lovely trattoria serves the kind of cooking that everyone wants to return to again and again. The slender room is instantly welcoming with its working pasta station and a whimsical portrait of Sophia Loren. The name (Italian for "pasta master") sets a very high bar but lives up to its moniker with a notable variety of hearty and elegant preparations listed as "classical" and "seasonal." Highlights have included soft, almost whipped polenta folded with showers of cacio e pepe and piled with fresh green peas and shaved pecorino. Spinach tonnarelli melded with a vibrantly seasoned lamb ragù exudes a faint whiff of sweetness.

Speaking of sweet, end with the wonderfully crumbly hazelnut cake with a delightful lemony edge.

4445 Connecticut Ave. NW (at Yuma St.)
Van Ness-UDC
(202) 450-1312 — **WEB:** www.sfoglinadc.com
Lunch Tue – Sun Dinner nightly

PRICE: $$

THE SMITH

Gastropub • Brasserie

MAP: 3-A3

The Smith, which boasts four locations in New York City, is a European brasserie decorated with basic wood furnishings, foxed mirror panels and sleek white-tiled walls. The warmly lit zinc bar showcases sparkling wine cocktails, punch and other drink specials like Moscow mules with house-made ginger beer. A tall communal table is ideal for gathering with friends.

The crowd-pleasing carte features a plethora of comfort food, like chicken pot pie, shellfish platters and mussels steamed in chardonnay. Lunchtime faves unveil rigatoni with wilted pea shoots and tomatoes dressed in parsley-almond pesto, while nightly specials culminate in a Saturday paella. Come on your special day for a slice of chocolate birthday cake, which is always on the menu.

901 F St. NW (at 9th St.)
Gallery Pl-Chinatown
(202) 868-4900 — **WEB:** www.thesmithrestaurant.com
Lunch & dinner daily

PRICE: $$

SIREN BY RW

Seafood • Elegant

With its gorgeous interior decked out in lush navy walls and supple leather banquettes, Robert Wiedmaier's beautiful Siren, at The Darcy hotel, is a sophisticated ode to elevated seafood. The menu keeps things simple, dividing its offerings into categories like raw, vegetables, fish and meat. For those looking to enliven things a touch, there is an excellent caviar service and tasting menu option.

Beyond the simple descriptions, the creative flourishes that dress each plate raise this kitchen's cooking to the next level. Attention to detail is evident from the start: perfectly prepared seafood platters boasting the freshest fish land on tables alongside dishes like the "Raw to Slightly Cooked" day boat scallop tiradito, coupled with a carrot- and Peruvian yellow pepper-dressing, kumquat and basil.

Meat options include the tender Shenandoah lamb saddle with jasmine dirty rice, charred okra, Virginia peanuts and lobster jus. Even vegetable sides are displayed with a striking aesthetic, as in the Vidalia onion brûlée, with country ham, pecans, blistered peppers and nori. Pescatarians will swoon over the perfectly executed salt-crusted branzino, stuffed with white fish mousse and finished with caviar crème.

■ 1515 Rhode Island Ave. NW (at Corregidor St.)

▦ Farragut North

✆ (202) 521-7171 — **WEB:** www.sirenbyrw.com

■ Lunch Sat – Sun Dinner nightly   PRICE: $$$

SOI 38

Thai • Elegant

MAP: 1-A3

Sidewalk seating is plentiful, but step inside Soi 38 and you'll discover a delightfully modern and elegant dining room. Black walls are emblazoned with gold-painted images, making a dramatic first impression. While the look is upscale, the menu celebrates the street foods of Thailand, offering a blend of influences from the owners' native Bangkok and the chef's Northern Thai heritage.

Settle in to a tall, curvy booth with a pile of friends and be sure to order gaeng hang lay, a tasty pork belly stew and the nam prik ong, a fun DIY lettuce wrap dish. Kua kling is a ground pork curry served with cucumber and green beans over rice; while seua rong hai is that holy grail of expertly grilled flank steak coupled with a spicy and crunchy green papaya salad.

2101 L St. NW (entrance on 21st St.)

Farragut North

(202) 558-9215 — **WEB:** www.soi38dc.com

Lunch & dinner daily

PRICE: **$$**

SONOMA

Contemporary • Wine bar

MAP: 4-A1

Located diagonally across from the Library of Congress, Sonoma serves as a water cooler of sorts for Capitol Hill staffers. Of course, you'll need to swap that water for wine, but with a lengthy by-the-glass selection, that won't be a problem. Despite the name, bottles aren't limited to California but hail from all over the world, including France, Italy and Spain. Want a little snack with your sip? There's plenty to choose from, with pâté de campagne, chicken liver mousse and Prosciutto Di Parma. Delicately fried Virginia oysters are served with a sweet Anaheim pepper purée and crumbly bits of bacon jam.

If happy hour drinks lead to dinner, more substantial dishes like lamb pappardelle and pan-seared rainbow trout are sure to fit the bill.

223 Pennsylvania Ave. SE (bet. Independence Ave. & 3rd St.)

Capitol South

(202) 544-8088 — **WEB:** www.sonomadc.com

Lunch Sun – Fri Dinner nightly

PRICE: **$$**

THE SOURCE BY WOLFGANG PUCK

Fusion • Chic

MAP: 3-B4

It would be, well, fake news to say that Wolfgang Puck's Asian cooking is authentic, but that's not why you dine at one of his restaurants. You're here to sample the food of a globe-trotting chef, who enjoys crafting his own interpretations of Pan-Asian dishes.

Tour the Newseum first; then settle in to a mustard-hued booth inside this elegant glass-walled space. One glance at a nearby table and you'll see that Puck's signature Chinese chicken salad hasn't lost any of its luster. Duck khao soi is also hearty and satisfying, but don't bury the lede by skipping dessert. The 15-layer carrot cake, with its distinct tiers of smooth crème cheese and carrot cake, served with ginger ice cream and candied walnuts in a crème anglaise, is absolutely superb.

■ 575 Pennsylvania Ave. NW (at 6th St.)
 Archives
✆ (202) 637-6100 — **WEB:** www.wolfgangpuck.com
■ Lunch Tue – Fri Dinner Tue – Sat   PRICE: $$$

THE SOVEREIGN

Belgian • Tavern

MAP: 6-B2

First you have to find it and it's a wonder anyone does—down an alley off the main drag—but when you do you most certainly won't want to leave. This beloved Georgetown standby is supremely handsome in that dark wood, red leather chair and wooden bench kind of way.

Sink into a cozy booth upstairs before perusing the Belgian beer list, which can be dizzying due to its variety, not including the 50 selections on draft. But a cheat sheet divvies them up into categories like tart + funky, roasted or crisp for a handy twist. The food is a perfect complement to these sips. A platter of meat and cheese makes for a hearty start, while mains like the mussels marinière are a must. The Sovereign burger spread with a brown beer-onion jam is yet another sure strike.

■ 1206 Wisconsin Ave. NW (bet. M & Prospect Sts.)
✆ (202) 774-5875 — **WEB:** www.thesovereigndc.com
■ Lunch Fri – Sun Dinner nightly   PRICE: $$

SPARK

Barbecue · Family

 ♿ ⛱ 🛋

MAP: 2-D4

Set within the historic Engine Company 12 firehouse, Spark is the lovechild of a good old-fashioned smokehouse and Caribbean spot. Come here hungry as there are many winning items and it would be a crime to limit yourself.

Start with that fry bread served with a trio of toppings, like curried chickpeas, spicy mango chutney and cucumber-red onion relish. Then move on to the tender lacquered chicken, fried three times, or guava-rum oxtail that is marinated for 48 hours and gets at the very soul of this place. Tamarind grilled lamb ribs are a hit, while Wagyu tri-tip in black garlic sauce takes a quality product and delivers next-level flavor. You may even find yourself spooning up bits of mango chow chow long after your stomach has waved the white flag.

🔲 1626 N Capitol St. NW (bet. Quincy Pl. & R St.)

📞 (202) 299-9128 — **WEB:** www.sparkat12.com

🔲 Lunch Tue – Sun Dinner Tue – Sat   PRICE: $$

SPOKEN ENGLISH 😃

Contemporary · Intimate

MAP: 2-A3

If you can't stand the heat, you can't get out of this kitchen, since Spoken English is standing room-only and you're practically right up against the stoves. Still, close quarters mean you'll be alongside the chefs as they prep dishes like whole-roast duck with crisp skin and matched by a delicious confit salad.

The menu centers around small plates and a wood-burning oven, out of which comes Wagyu short rib or grilled camembert glazed with fermented honey and smoked olive oil. Creativity runs rampant, especially in the dumpling made from fried chicken skin and stuffed with sausage, shrimp and salt cod; or the daring-but-delightful durian curry over spaghetti squash with all of the creamy, tropical flavor and none of the legendary off-putting odor.

🔲 1770 Euclid St. NW (at Columbia Rd. NW)

🚇 Woodley-Park Zoo

📞 (202) 588-0525 — **WEB:** www.thelinehotel.com

🔲 Lunch Tue – Sat   PRICE: $$

STABLE DC ⬥

European • *Rustic*

MAP: 8-C4

When the temperatures dip, head straight for Stable. Transporting diners to the Alps, this warming and proud pearl is replete with exposed wood beams, cozy lighting and Swiss flags. It exudes that classic Alpine lodge feel, even if you're more aprés-office than aprés-ski.

Stable is the city's first and only Swiss retreat, so arrive with a crew to tuck into raclette fondue—with boiled new potatoes, topped with cheese and coupled with cornichons. Cream, butter and starch are the soul of this kitchen, not the exception, so don't expect a light meal. Having said that, veal Zurich in a mushroom-cream sauce is hearty enough to chase the chills away. Garnished with fried onions, cheese spaetzli then forms the very picture of comfort food through and through.

▪ 1324 H St. (bet. 13th St. & Wylie Ct.)
☎ (202) 733-4604 — **WEB:** www.stabledc.com
▪ Lunch Sat – Sun Dinner Tue – Sun   **PRICE:** $$

SUCCOTASH ☺

Southern • *Historic*

MAP: 3-A3

A Brooklynite plating some of the best Southern cooking this side of the Mason-Dixon line—no it's not a punch line; it's Edward Lee's Succotash. This gem bucks all stereotypes, so before you arrive thinking it's a red-and-white checkered tablecloth sort of spot, think again. It is nestled inside a former bank, and features soaring ceilings, Corinthian columns and mahogany paneling.

Good looks aside, diners come for their sensational food, known for its extra oomph. The Kentucky country ham board with biscuits and aged ham makes for a fine start. Then pimento cheese is amplified with Worcestershire for next-level flavor. Finally, make way for that chocolate-Bourbon pecan pie, replete with all of the intensity and richness of a molten lava cake.

▪ 915 F St. NW (bet. F & G Sts.)
🚇 Metro Center
☎ (202) 849-6933 — **WEB:** www.succotashrestaurant.com
▪ Lunch & dinner daily   **PRICE:** $$

SUPRA 😳

Eastern European • *Contemporary décor*

MAP: 3-A1

Georgian food is having a moment, so head to Supra to dine on this deeply satisfying cuisine (make reservations; it's popular). The dining room's dark wood paneling and gleaming wood tables lean elegant, while the iconic puffy sheep hats hanging in the entrance flaunt regional flair.

This chef once ran the kitchen at the same nation's Embassy, so expect authenticity with a dose of delicious. Start with the house platter, a panoply of spreads and cheeses with warm bread for dipping, before devouring soup dumplings or a plate of mussels. No diner worth his or her salt would dare skip their classic khachapuri—a stuffed, turtle-shaped crusty bread with a pit of molten cheese and runny egg.

Thirsty travelers should explore the Georgian-focused wine list.

▨ 1205 11th St. NW (bet. M & N Sts.)
🚇 McPherson Square
☏ (202) 789-1205 — **WEB:** www.supradc.com
▨ Lunch Tue – Sun Dinner nightly   PRICE: $$

SUSHI OGAWA 🍴

Japanese • *Minimalist*

MAP: 2-A4

Tokyo-born Minoru Ogawa is running something of a mini-empire with Sushi Capitol, Mirai and the sushi counter at the Mandarin Oriental. But, Sushi Ogawa is his namesake and the most intimate (there are just seven seats at the counter). The interior design is clean and contemporary, with warm accents of honey wood.

Omakase is always the preferred manner of business here, however, be ready as it comes out at lightning-speed and the litany of nigiri delivered your way may just make you vertiginous. Sashimi, often blowtorched, may include Spanish mackerel, tuna, clam or sea trout with scallions; while the nigiri follows a rhythm and flow from simple to complex. The itamae listen closely and might even throw in a few extra pieces of your favorite fish.

▨ 2100 Connecticut Ave. NW (Kalorama Rd. & Wyoming Ave.)
🚇 Dupont Circle
☏ (202) 813-9715 — **WEB:** www.sushiogawa.com
▨ Lunch Mon – Fri Dinner Mon – Sat   PRICE: $$$$

SUSHI TARO ✿

Japanese • Intimate

MAP: 1-C1

Sushi aficionados know to give this beloved Dupont Circle gem a pass for its odd location—adjacent to a large-chain pharmacy and accessed by a short flight of steps. However, the interior then opens up into a comfortable and warmly attended dining room. Sushi Taro may offer a solid à la carte and numerous tasting menus, but the overall experience at the omakase counter is truly stellar.

Scoring a meal at said counter proves challenging since seats can only be booked online, via e-mail, 30 days in advance. Once secured, a reservation here grants entrée to a cloistered room where Chefs Nobu Yamazaki and Masaya Kitayama cater to a mere handful of diners.

Following the construct of kaiseki, the meal is a series of artistically composed courses, such as grilled marinated tuna cheek or squid ink-tinted soft-shell crab tempura. The experience hits its apex come sushi time when the chefs present a stack of boxes stocked with an immense selection of fish arranged by type, and then invite diners to make selections from this bounty, which are then knifed into sashimi. An equally superb nigiri course follows, allowing further opportunity to delve deeper into the jaw-dropping assemblage.

▪ 1503 17th St. NW (bet. Church & P Sts.)

▪ Dupont Circle

✆ (202) 462-8999 — **WEB:** www.sushitaro.com

▪ Lunch Mon – Fri Dinner Mon – Sat　　　　　**PRICE: $$$$**

TABARD INN

American • Historic

MAP: 1-C2

Nestled amidst a row of brownstones, Tabard Inn's library-like entrance—complete with handsome wooden floors and historic decorations—befits a restaurant that first opened in 1922. But, you can also bet your grandmother's china that this kitchen didn't serve shish kebabs or paella back then. They do now, of course, and this gem that is tucked inside DC's oldest continuously operated hotel doesn't adhere to any rules.

It's a place where American food like fried Virginia oysters, seared duck breast and filet mignon mingle with Middle Eastern-minded items. Envision the likes of grilled lamb sausage on a bed of lentils; or Palestinian "pasta" stuffed with ground beef and set in a yogurt- and pomegranate seed-sauce—a specialty of the chef's mother.

 1739 N St. NW (bet. 17th & 18th Sts.)
Dupont Circle
(202) 331-8528 — **WEB:** www.tabardinn.com
Lunch & dinner daily　　　　　**PRICE:** $$

TABERNA DEL ALABARDERO

Spanish • Contemporary décor

MAP: 1-B4

When times call for unapologetic, old-world formality, reserve a table at Taberna del Albardero. Regal and resplendent, with everything from the walls and fabrics to the plush carpets awash in vivid red, this is the kind of place where servers donning formal attire deliver white glove service to international dignitaries—the din of a dozen different languages weaving a kind of symphony in the background.

Madrid-native Javier Romero's menu begins with classic Spanish tapas—patatas bravas and gambas al ajillo. Edgier creations may include prawn burgers on ink-tinted buns and arroz cremosa calabaza, a Spanish riff on risotto with tempura-fried Blue Point oysters, butternut squash purée-flavored sauce and a drizzle of anise liqueur.

1776 I St. NW (entrance on 18th St.)
Farragut North
(202) 429-2200 — **WEB:** www.alabardero.com
Lunch Mon – Fri Dinner nightly　　　　**PRICE:** $$$

TAIL UP GOAT

Contemporary · Chic

MAP: 2-A3

When three alums of Komi and Little Serow combine their talents, the result is bound to be an easygoing favorite, where food, drinks and hospitality mesh effortlessly. The mood here is buzzy and the interior colorful, with watery blue murals and highly attentive servers. Don't be fooled by the casual vibe though, as this kitchen is notably serious.

Tables are filled with dates or celebrants, all leaning over shared plates of Mediterranean specialties. Starters have included the spice-rubbed and gently sweet barbecue carrots, bearing just a hint of hickory smoke. Be sure to indulge in clever bread courses, like red fife sourdough rubbed in "burnt bread sauce" and brightened by lightly dressed lettuce. Pastas are equally popular in this dining room, especially the delicate triangoli draped with pea-shoot pesto. Do not, under any circumstances, skip their show-stopping signature dish—lamb ribs dressed in date-molasses jus, with such juicy and smoky meat that it nearly slides off the bone.

A wall of wine bottles frames the semi-open kitchen, showcasing a list of interesting pours ranging from Georgia to Greece. During dessert, don't forget to inquire about their vintage Madeira and Port.

■ 1827 Adams Mill Rd. NW (bet. Lanier Pl. & Columbia Rd.)

✆ (202) 986-9600 — **WEB:** www.tailupgoat.com

■ Dinner nightly

PRICE: $$

THAI X-ING

Thai • Cozy

MAP: 2-C4

Climb the creaky wooden stairs and take your seat among a homey hodgepodge of chairs and tables. If it feels like someone's house, that's the point (you'll pour your own water, too). There's no menu to bother with, so settle in with your pals and prepare yourself for a parade of Thai dishes that satisfy hungry patrons without breaking the bank.

Feast on up to ten different dishes, ranging from dumplings, green papaya salad and pork skewers, before delving into the kitchen's signature pumpkin curry. The tender pumpkin cubes bobbing in a red curry balances its sweetness without ever tasting like dessert. Tom yum soup is another crowd-pleaser with shrimp as well as a zippy lime and fish sauce. Mango coconut sticky rice closes out the night on a tropical note.

 2020 9th St. NW (at Florida Ave.)

Shaw-Howard U

(202) 332-4322 — **WEB:** www.thaix-ing.com

Dinner Tue – Sun **PRICE:** $$

THIP KHAO

Lao • Neighborhood

MAP: 2-B1

Having earned herself a loyal following at Bangkok Golden in Falls Church, Chef Seng Luangrath continues to wow crowds in ever-transforming Columbia Heights.

Thip Khao's menu tempts with its sheer variety, from snacks and salads to soups, curries and a panoply of entrées. Naem khao, a crispy coconut rice salad, bursts with fresh and fragrant flavor, while muu som, cured and slow-cooked pork belly, is wonderfully fatty. Crispy pig ears dusted with a deliciously tart tamarind salt and dipped in fermented chili-fish sauce are both original and outstanding, but the knap paa, or Chilean sea bass, is a true standout. Brushed with curry paste and coconut cream, then grilled in a banana leaf, this dish will have you wondering if it's dinner or a present?

3462 14th St. NW (bet. Meridian Pl. & Newton St.)

Columbia Heights

(202) 387-5426 — **WEB:** www.thipkao.com

Lunch Fri – Sun Dinner Wed– Mon **PRICE:** $$

TICO ⭐🍽

Latin American • *Colorful*

MAP: 2-B4

It may be an offshoot of the Boston original, but Tico stands on its own two feet. Pulsing with energy, it fits right in with this lively U Street neighborhood. The spacious dining room's dark wood furnishings and vibrant murals create the sense of relaxing in a Latin American courtyard—and once those hibiscus margaritas arrive, stress has no chance.

Lunch is mainly tacos, but come dinner, the small plates menu offers plenty to choose from, including ceviche (snapper is especially good); guacamole with an inventive sprinkle of black olive powder; and cauliflower roasted and covered in crunchy fava beans and cotija cheese. From Spanish octopus with panca vinaigrette to Brussels sprouts with aji lime honey, the items cooked a la plancha are always a hit.

 1926 14th St. NW (bet. T & U Sts.)

 U St

✆ (202) 319-1400 — **WEB:** www.ticodc.com

Lunch Sat – Sun Dinner nightly　　　　**PRICE:** $$

TIGER FORK 😀

Chinese • *Trendy*

MAP: 3-A1

Tiger Fork feels secreted away. Indeed, its location off the main road makes finding it a challenge, but arrive and discover a sultry Hong Kong-style den. Inside, find brick walls emblazoned with dragons and mountains, Chinese basket-style lanterns, and warehouse floors that show off a sexy, hip look. Then get to sipping on one of their many glorious potions, such as the Bird Market, a chartreuse blended with elderflower, bai zhu and bergamot.

Some plates may miss the mark but dishes like the slightly sweet cheung fun or beef chow chow are spot on. Chairman's clams are a bowl of umami glory, with an intensely briny broth. Crack open that fortune cookie but don't expect Confucius since you're more likely to get words of wisdom from Gucci Mane.

922 N St. NW (entrance on Blagden Alley)

✆ (202) 733-1152 — **WEB:** www.tigerforkdc.com

Lunch Sat – Sun Dinner nightly　　　　**PRICE:** $$

TIMBER PIZZA CO

Pizza • *Rustic*

MAP: 2-C1

It may be the signature cry for falling objects, but Timber Pizza Co is only on its way up. This popular neighborhood hangout is on a mounting spiral after transitioning from a farmer's market fave to a brick-and-mortar crowd magnet that also boasts a booming takeout business.

So what's all the fuss about? It's the flavorful cooking, of course. A few bites into the Griffin salad and it's clear this kitchen knows how to handle itself. Those in the know order a half and half to explore the wide variety of pizzas. The D&D's mix of za'atar, finely diced sweet peppers and garlic chips is inventively delicious; while The Hughes piles bacon, cherry tomatoes, jalapeños and basil atop a white cheese pie slathered with a subtle and sweet tomato sauce.

- 809 Upshur St. NW (bet. 8th & 9th Sts.)
- Georgia Ave-Petworth
- (202) 853-9746 — **WEB:** www.timberpizza.com
- Lunch Sat– Sun Dinner Tue– Sun

PRICE: 🍴

TOKI UNDERGROUND 👻

Japanese • *Simple*

MAP: 8-C4

You'll go up the stairs, not down to Toki Underground, which shares the same front door as The Pug Bar. Once inside, notice raw wood beams, walls plastered with stickers and scribble, as well as dangling Christmas lights that exude a sense of childlike angst. That angst may grow into full-blown annoyance though as the waits are staggeringly long (there are just 30 counter seats and no tables), but come for lunch to steer clear of all lines.

Fried chicken steamed buns; lightly battered and delicately fried enoki mushrooms; or pork dumplings are a good way to start things off. The Toki classic with chasu pork and a soft egg is a signature dish, where the broth is slurp-worthy. Its stick-to-your-bones porky intensity is especially memorable.

- 1234 H St. NE (bet. 12th & 13th Sts.)
- (202) 388-3086 — **WEB:** www.tokiunderground.com
- Lunch & dinner Mon – Sat

PRICE: 🍴

TOSCA

Italian • *Elegant*

MAP: 3-A3

Tosca pulls off a bit of a magic trick, as you'd never suspect that this gem was hiding in plain sight. Shielded by an unassuming façade, it's more than easy to walk right by. But what a shame that would be as the elegant dining room, awash in soft cream and gray tones and flowing drapes, pulls off a few throwbacks (a carpet!) with aplomb.

Lunch brings in an army of suits to match those starched white tablecloths and deals are done over platters of house-made pasta. Trevigiana, a salad tossing bright radicchio with crispy hen of the woods mushrooms, frico friulano and a piquant black truffle dressing, shows restraint and focus; while lobster risotto with its sweet tomato bisque and tender Maine lobster meat exudes a harmony of decadent flavors.

1112 F St. NW (bet. 11th & 12th Sts.)
Metro Center
(202) 367-1990 — **WEB:** www.toscadc.com
Lunch Mon – Fri Dinner Mon – Sat   PRICE: $$$

UNCONVENTIONAL DINER

American • *Family*

MAP: 3-B1

With its white walls and seafoam-green booths, this "diner" may look like the classic American translation, but is in fact a far cry from your tuna-melt standby. Instead, this kitchen ramps up known classics by riffing on tradition. Need proof? Look no further than the kale nachos. Likewise, meatloaf is elevated with a hint of spicy sriracha and an earthy morel mushroom gravy; while even an expert fishmonger wouldn't recognize those fish sticks enhanced with saffron aïoli. Roasted cauliflower tossed in tahini with fried chickpeas for crunch and pickled red onions for acidity is yet another win and goes to show that creating new traditions here is just as vital as jazzing up the old ones.

For salads and sammies during the day, visit its casual café.

 1207 9th St. (bet. N & M Sts.)
McPherson Sq
(202) 847-0122 — **WEB:** www.unconventionaldiner.com
Lunch Sat– Sun Dinner nightly   PRICE: $$

WHALEY'S

Seafood · *Trendy*

            MAP: 4-A4

From its Navy Yard location with floor-to-ceiling windows that overlook the Anacostia River, to its playful interior design featuring a giant curtain mimicking a ship's sail as well as ocean murals, there is no mistaking that Whaley's is all about seafood. In fact, it's the kind of refuge where one comes to slurp away oyster after oyster. The oceanic flavors present in a nasturtium shrimp taco with a charred tomatillo sauce and creamy yuzu kosho is so satisfying you might want to go for two...or twenty. Smoked blue catfish topped with slivers of Benton bacon and spread over toasted bread marries its charred goodness with just the right amount of crunch.

Dining à deux? The seafood risotto, with its unexpected hits of pickled Fresno chilies, is faultless.

301 Water St. SE (in Yards Park)
(202) 484-8800 — **WEB:** www.whaleysdc.com
Lunch Sat – Sun Dinner nightly   PRICE: $$

ZAYTINYA

Mediterranean · *Contemporary décor*

     **MAP:** 3-B3

Powerhouse chef José Andrés' ocean-blue ode to the foods of Greece, Lebanon and Turkey means the mezze menu ranges far and wide, from flatbreads to kebabs to dips. Greek and Lebanese wines are given their fair due on the exceptional wine list.

Zaytinya speaks to the ease and elegance of the Mediterranean—zero in on the grape leaves, garides me anitho and the Turkish braised lamb that tastes like the Sunday roast everyone deserves. The dishes show refinement and skill while still coming off as immensely personal.

Despite the size, the large dining room is sectioned into cozy nooks; solo diners should head to the long bar. The warm service makes it feel especially inviting, likely accounting for the perpetual crowd (so make reservations).

701 9th St. NW (at G St.)
Gallery Pl-Chinatown
(202) 638-0800 — **WEB:** www.zaytinya.com
Lunch & dinner daily   PRICE: $$

MAPS

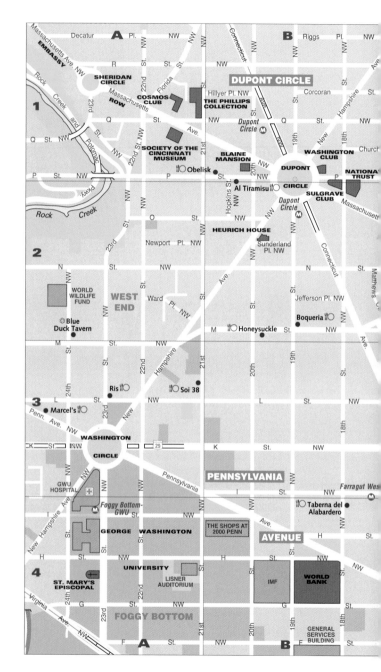

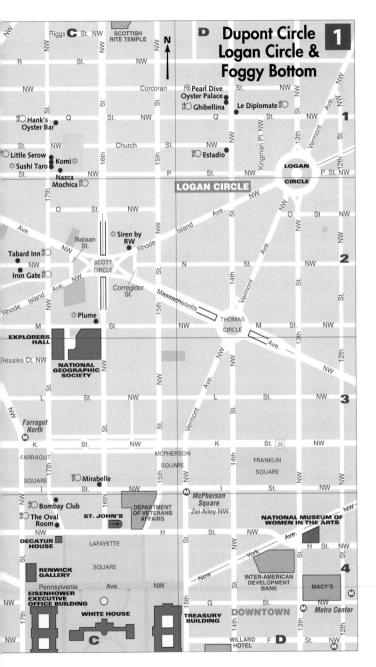

Riggs **C** St. NW

SCOTTISH RITE TEMPLE

N

R St. NW

NW

Corcoran St. NW

Pearl Dive Oyster Palace

NW

Ghibellina

Le Diplomate

Hank's Oyster Bar

Q St. NW

Q St. NW

Kingman Pl. NW

13th St.

Vermont Ave.

St. NW

Church St. NW

Little Serow

Komi

Estadio

Sushi Taro

St. NW

Nazca

Mochica

P St. NW

P St. NW

LOGAN CIRCLE

LOGAN CIRCLE

O St. NW

O St. NW

Ave.

St.

Island Ave.

Tabard Inn

Siren by RW

Bataan St.

Rhode

N St. NW

NW

Ave.

St.

Iron Gate

SCOTT CIRCLE

2

Rhode Island

Ave.

NW

Corregidor St.

Massachusetts

Vermont St.

THOMAS CIRCLE

12th St.

Plume

M St. NW

13th St.

EXPLORERS HALL

Ave.

NW

Desales Ct. NW

NATIONAL GEOGRAPHIC SOCIETY

NW

St.

12th

L St. NW

L St. NW

3

Farragut North

St.

St.

Vermont St.

K St. NW

K St. 29 NW

FARRAGUT SQUARE

MCPHERSON SQUARE

14th St.

FRANKLIN SQUARE

17th St.

Mirabelle

St. NW

St. NW

SQUARE

St. NW

Bombay Club

16th St.

McPherson Square

NW

The Oval Room

ST. JOHN'S

DEPARTMENT OF VETERANS AFFAIRS

Zei Alley NW

NATIONAL MUSEUM OF WOMEN IN THE ARTS

DECATUR HOUSE

NW

LAFAYETTE

H St. NW

Ave.

H St. NW

4

St.

St.

SQUARE

York

New

St.

13th St.

RENWICK GALLERY

INTER-AMERICAN DEVELOPMENT BANK

MACY'S

Pennsylvania Ave. NW

EISENHOWER EXECUTIVE OFFICE BUILDING

15th St.

G St. NW

DOWNTOWN

Metro Center

17th St.

WHITE HOUSE

C

TREASURY BUILDING

14th St.

13th St.

12th

NW

NW

WILLARD HOTEL

F **D** St. NW

2

ROCK CREEK PARK AND
PINEY BRANCH PARKWAY

Branch

Piney   Rd.

Park   Pkwy.

JC

Beach

1

Ingleside   Terr.   NW

Newton   St.   NW

Klingle   Rd.

19th   St.

Park   St.

Adams   Mill

**MT.
PLEASANT**

Mt. Pleasant St. NW

Brown   St.

Meridian

Monroe

Newton

St.

NW

St.

NW

Spring

Rd.   NW

Spring   Pl.   NW

Ogden   St.

Perry   Pl.

14th   St.

NW

Quincy

Otis   Pl

NW

B

🕎 **Thip Khao**   NW

Holmead

Beach   Dr.

North   Rd.

Klingle

⬧ **SMITHSONIAN**

▯ **NATIONAL**

2   **ZOOLOGICAL**

PARK

Rock Creek

🍽 **Ellé**

Lamont   St.

🕎 **Mola**

🍽 **Purple Patch**

18th   St.

Kenyon   St.

Irving   St.   NW

Hobart   St.   NW

17th   St.   NW

Harvard   St.   NW

Mill   Rd.   NW

16th   St.

15th   St.

Park   Rd.

Pleasant

Powell

Meridian   Pl.

Monroe

St.

NW

NW

Park

**GALA
(TIVOLI
THEATER)**

**POWELL
RECREATION
CENTER**

Kenyon

St.

**Columbia
Heights**

Ⓜ   Irving

Columbia   Rd.

St.

Ontario   Rd.   NW

Mill   Rd.   NW

Dr.   NW

Rock Creek

Adams   Mill   Rd.

Ontario   Pl.   NW

Lanier   Pl.   NW

Columbia   Rd.

Fuller   St.   NW

17th   St.   NW

**RABAUT
PARK**

Harvard   St.

**MEXICAN
CULTURAL
INSTITUTE**

Girard

**COLUMBIA
HEIGHTS
PARK**

COLUMBIA HEIGHTS

**WALTER PIERCE
PARK**

Calvert   St.

Biltmore   St.

Beach

🌸 **Tail Up Goat**

🍽 **A Rake's
Progress**

🕎 **Spoken
English**   ●●

St.   NW

🍽 **Mintwood Place**

🕎 **Lapis**

Mintwood Pl.

20th   St.

**KALORAMA
PARK**

ADAMS

The Diner 🍽

🍽 **Sakuramen**

18th   St.

Euclid   St.

Ontario   Rd.

16th   St.

Belmont Rd.
NW

MORGAN

19th   St.
NW

Champlain   St.

Kalorama   Rd.

Clifton

Chapin   St.   NW

**MERIDIAN
HILL
PARK**

Belmont St.   NW

Florida

🕎 **Maydān**   Ave.

🍽 **Kapnos**   ●   NW

Connecticut

Kalorama

Wyoming St. NW

Belmont St.

NW

NW

W   St.

NW

14th

🍽 **Sushi Ogawa**

Wyoming   Ave.   NW

California   St.   NW

California   St.   NW

Phelps Pl. NW

Leroy Pl.   NW

4

Bancroft Pl.
NW

Decatur Pl. NW

**MARIE
REED
RECR.
CTR.**

Columbia   Rd.

Vernon St.   NW

🍽 **Keren**

T   St.

19th   St.

20th   Ave.

Swann   St.

Mandu 🍽

NW

Riggs   Pl.

18th   St.

Florida

Florida

California

**Jack Rose
Dining Saloon** 🍽

Willard   St.   NW

NW

Swann   St.

17th   St.
NW

New   Hampshire

16th   St.

A

S   St.

V   St.

U   St.

NW

NW

NW

NW

Ave.

NW

Swann

S   St.

NW

Riggs Pl

15th   St.

🍽 **Tico**   ●

🌸 **Bresca**   ●

🍽 **Lupo Verde**   St.

T   St.

🕎 **Doi Moi**   NW

NW

14th   St.

B

NW

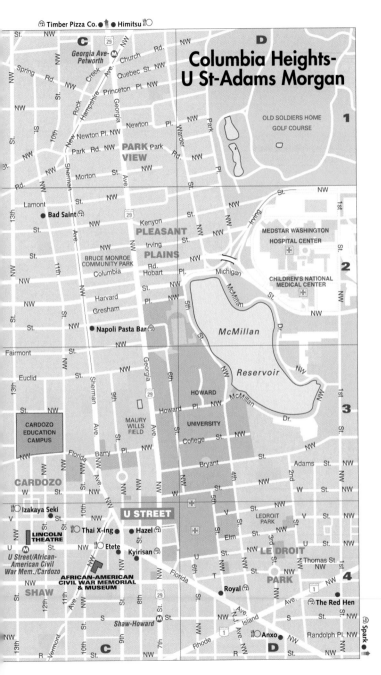

Timber Pizza Co. ● ▮ ● Himitsu ▮○

Columbia Heights-
U St-Adams Morgan

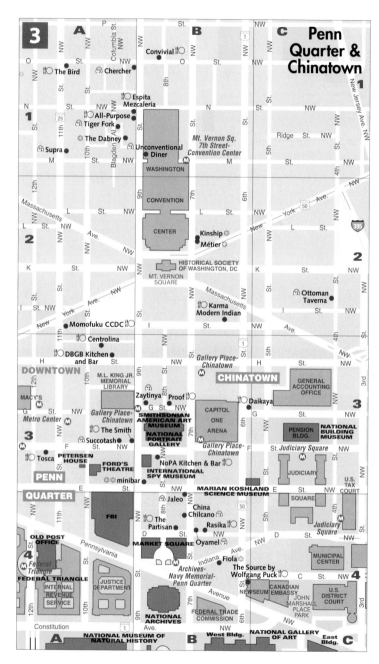

3 Penn Quarter & Chinatown

A

Columbia St.
P St.
O St. NW
The Bird
Chercher
N St. NW
Espita Mezcaleria
All-Purpose
Tiger Fork
The Dabney
Supra
Unconventional Diner

11th St.
Blagden Al.
10th St.
M St. NW
29

Massachusetts Ave. NW
12th St.
L St. NW
K St.
New York Ave. NW
I St. NW
Momofuku CCDC
Centrolina
DBGB Kitchen and Bar

DOWNTOWN

M.L. KING JR. MEMORIAL LIBRARY
MACY'S
Metro Center
Gallery Place-Chinatown
Zaytinya
Proof
The Smith
Succotash
SMITHSONIAN AMERICAN ART MUSEUM
NATIONAL PORTRAIT GALLERY

PENN

Tosca
PETERSEN HOUSE
FORD'S THEATRE
minibar
INTERNATIONAL SPY MUSEUM

QUARTER

Jaleo
The Partisan
FBI
OLD POST OFFICE
Federal Triangle
FEDERAL TRIANGLE
INTERNAL REVENUE SERVICE
JUSTICE DEPARTMENT
Pennsylvania
MARKET SQUARE
China Chilcano
Rasika
Oyamel
Indiana Ave.
Fiola
Archives-Navy Memorial-Penn Quarter
NATIONAL ARCHIVES
FEDERAL TRADE COMMISSION
Constitution Ave.

B

Convivial
8th St. NW
Mt. Vernon Sq. 7th Street-Convention Center
WASHINGTON
CONVENTION
CENTER
Kinship
Métier
HISTORICAL SOCIETY OF WASHINGTON, DC
MT. VERNON SQUARE
Massachusetts Ave. NW
New York Ave. NW
Karma Modern Indian
Gallery Place-Chinatown
CHINATOWN
CAPITOL ONE ARENA
Daikaya
Gallery Place-Chinatown
NoPA Kitchen & Bar
MARIAN KOSHLAND SCIENCE MUSEUM
7th St.
The Source by Wolfgang Puck
NEWSEUM
7th Avenue
West Bldg.
NATIONAL MUSEUM OF NATURAL HISTORY
NATIONAL GALLERY OF ART

C

Penn Quarter & Chinatown

New Jersey Ave. NW
Ridge St. NW
5th St.
New York Ave. 50
395
Ottoman Taverna
4th St.
GENERAL ACCOUNTING OFFICE
3rd St.
PENSION BLDG.
NATIONAL BUILDING MUSEUM
Judiciary Square
JUDICIARY
U.S. TAX COURT
SQUARE
Judiciary Square
MUNICIPAL CENTER
CANADIAN EMBASSY
JOHN MARSHALL PLACE PARK
U.S. DISTRICT COURT
East Bldg.

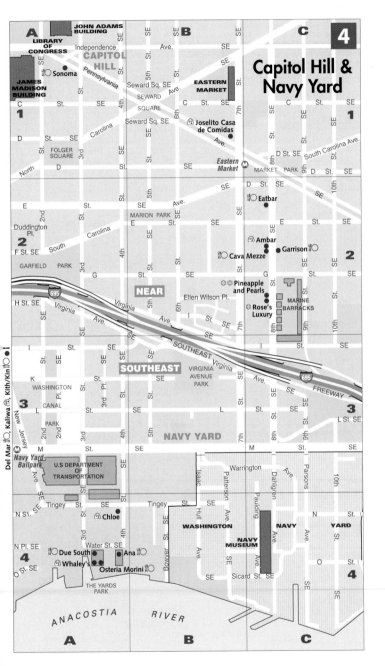

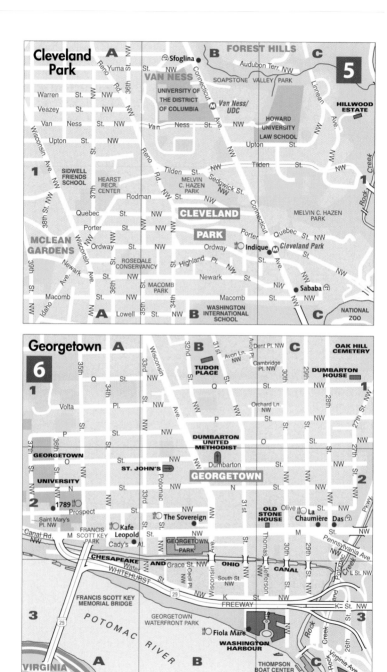

Cleveland Park

A Yuma St.

B FOREST HILLS

C 5

Reno Rd.

36th St. NW

Sfoglina

Audubon Terr. NW

VAN NESS

SOAPSTONE VALLEY PARK

UNIVERSITY OF
THE DISTRICT
OF COLUMBIA

Van Ness/
UDC

Connecticut

Linnean

Warren St. NW

Veazey St. NW

Van Ness St. NW

HOWARD
UNIVERSITY
LAW SCHOOL

HILLWOOD
ESTATE

Ave.

Wisconsin Ave. NW

Upton St. NW

Van Ness St. NW

Upton St.

1 SIDWELL
FRIENDS
SCHOOL

HEARST
RECR.
CENTER

Tilden St. NW

Tilden St. NW

1

37th St. NW

Reno Rd. NW

Sedgwick St. NW

MELVIN
C. HAZEN
PARK

Connecticut

Rock Creek

Rodman St. NW

38th St. NW

Quebec St. NW

CLEVELAND

MELVIN C. HAZEN
PARK

Porter St. NW

PARK

Porter St.

Quebec St. NW

MCLEAN
GARDENS

39th St. NW

Wisconsin

Ordway St. NW

Ordway St.

Indique

Cleveland Park

Ave.

NW

ROSEDALE
CONSERVANCY

36th St.

Highland Pl. NW

Newark St.

Sababa

Newark St. NW

34th St.

MACOMB
PARK

Macomb St.

NATIONAL
ZOO

Idaho Ave. NW

Macomb St. NW

A Lowell St. NW

35th St.

34th St.

B WASHINGTON
INTERNATIONAL
SCHOOL

C

Georgetown

A 35th

B 31st

32nd

Avon Pl. NW

Dent Pl. NW

C OAK HILL
CEMETERY

6

Wisconsin

33rd

Q St.

TUDOR
PLACE

Avon Ln. NW

Cambridge Pl. NW

30th

29th

DUMBARTON
HOUSE

1

34th Pl.

St. NW

St. NW

28th

1

Volta Pl.

33rd St. NW

Q St. NW

P St.

Orchard Ln. NW

27th St. NW

P St.

NW

36th St. NW

37th St. NW

GEORGETOWN

O St. NW

DUMBARTON
UNITED
METHODIST

O St.

St. NW

UNIVERSITY

N St. NW

ST. JOHN'S

Dumbarton St.

GEORGETOWN

St. NW

NW

2 1789

Prospect St.

33rd St. NW

N St.

31st St.

N St. NW

27th St. NW

2

Saint Mary's
Pl. NW

The Sovereign

OLD
STONE
HOUSE

Olive St.

La
Chaumière

Das

FRANCIS
SCOTT KEY
PARK

Kafe
Leopold

Cady's Al.

M St.

Thomas Jefferson St.

M St. NW

Pennsylvania Ave. NW

Canal Rd. NW

GEORGETOWN
PARK

Wisconsin Ave.

OHIO

30th St.

29th St.

Rock Creek Pkwy.

L St. NW

CHESAPEAKE AND

Grace St. NW

CANAL

Potomac St.

WHITEHURST

Cecil Pl. NW

South St. NW

K St. NW

26th St.

FRANCIS SCOTT KEY
MEMORIAL BRIDGE

29

29 FREEWAY

3 POTOMAC

GEORGETOWN
WATERFRONT PARK

Fiola Mare

Rock Creek

K St. NW

3

VIRGINIA

RIVER

WASHINGTON
HARBOUR

THOMPSON
BOAT CENTER

Virginia Ave.

C

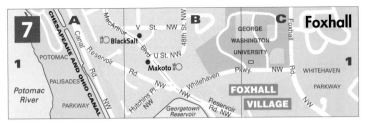

A
B
C

MacArthur Blvd.
V St. NW
48th St. NW
Foxhall Rd.

GEORGE
WASHINGTON
UNIVERSITY

Canal Reservoir

BlackSalt

POTOMAC

U St. NW

Pkwy. NW

WHITEHAVEN

1

Hutchins Pl. NW

Makoto

Whitehaven

FOXHALL

PARKWAY

Rd.

PALISADES

NW

VILLAGE

Potomac
River

PARKWAY

Georgetown
Reservoir

Reservoir
Rd. NW

NW

CHESAPEAKE AND OHIO CANAL

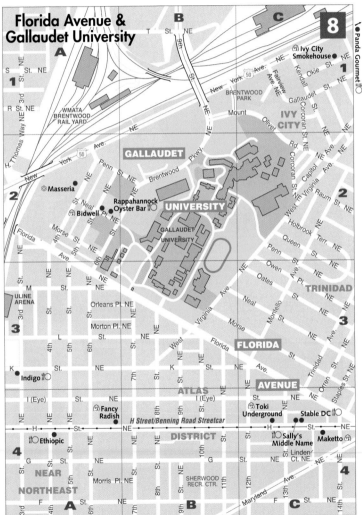

Florida Avenue &
Gallaudet University

B

T St. NE

9th St. NE

C

8

A

Ivy City
Smokehouse

Panda Gourmet

S St. NE

New York Ave.

Kendall St. NE

Okie St. NE

1

R St. NE

3rd St. NE

WMATA
BRENTWOOD
RAIL YARD

BRENTWOOD
PARK

Fairview Ave. NE

Corcoran St. NE

Gallaudet St.

NE

IVY
CITY

H. Thomas Way NE

New York Ave.

50

Mount

Olivet Rd.

NE

Corcoran St. NE

Capitol Ave. NE

West Virginia Ave. NE

Raum St. NE

Masseria

Penn St. NE

Brentwood Pkwy.

GALLAUDET

2

Neal Pl. NE

Rappahannock
Oyster Bar

UNIVERSITY

Holbrook Terr. NE

2

Bidwell

Morse St. NE

4th St. NE

5th St. NE

GALLAUDET
UNIVERSITY

Queen St. NE

Florida Ave. NE

6th St. NE

Penn St. NE

Owen Pl. NE

West Virginia Ave.

TRINIDAD

M St. NE

ULINE
ARENA

Orleans Pl. NE

Oates St. NE

Neal St. NE

Montello Ave. NE

3

3rd St. NE

L St. NE

Morton Pl. NE

West St. NE

Florida Ave.

Morse St. NE

3

4th St. NE

5th St. NE

6th St. NE

FLORIDA

Trinidad Ave. NE

K St. NE

7th St. NE

8th St. NE

K St. NE

AVENUE

Orren St. NE

Staples St. NE

Indigo

I (Eye) St. NE

I (Eye) St. NE

ATLAS

Toki
Underground

Stable DC

4

4th St. NE

5th St. NE

Fancy
Radish

8th St. NE

9th St. NE

H Street/Benning Road Streetcar

DISTRICT

Maketto

Ethiopic

NEAR

Morris Pl. NE

10th St.

G St. NE

11th St.

Sally's
Middle Name

Linden Ct. NE

Sally's

4

NORTHEAST

G St. NE

SHERWOOD
RECR. CTR.

12th St.

Maryland Ave. NE

F St. NE

13th St. NE

14th St.

F St. NE

3rd St.

4th St.

A

5th St.

6th St.

7th St.

B

8th St.

9th St.

C

INDEXES

ALPHABETICAL LIST OF RESTAURANTS

RESTAURANTS BY CUISINE

BARBECUE

BASQUE

BELGIAN

CHINESE

CONTEMPORARY

EASTERN EUROPEAN

ETHIOPIAN

EUROPEAN

FILIPINO

FRENCH

FUSION

GASTROPUB

GREEK

INDIAN

INTERNATIONAL

ITALIAN

JAPANESE

KOREAN

LAO

LATIN AMERICAN

MEDITERRANEAN

MEXICAN

MIDDLE EASTERN

PERUVIAN

PIZZA

SEAFOOD

SOUTHERN

SPANISH

THAI

TURKISH

VEGAN

STARRED
RESTAURANTS

BIB GOURMAND

UNDER $25

Tell us what you think about our products.

Give us your opinion

satisfaction.michelin.com

CREDITS

NOV 2 7 2018

MICHELIN TRAVEL PARTNER

Société par actions simplifiées au capital de 15 044 940 EUR
27 Cours de l'Ile Seguin - 92100 Boulogne Billancourt (France)
R.C.S. Nanterre 433 677 721

© 2018 Michelin Travel Partner - All rights reserved
Dépôt légal august 2018
Printed in Canada - august 2018
Printed on paper from sustainably managed forests

Impression et Finition : Transcontinental (Canada)

EYEWITNESS *TRAVEL GUIDES*

ITALIAN
PHRASE BOOK

DORLING KINDERSLEY
LONDON • NEW YORK • STUTTGART • MOSCOW

A DORLING KINDERSLEY BOOK

Compiled by Lexus Ltd with Karen McAulay
and Mariarosaria Cardines

Set in 9/9 Plantin and Plantin Light by Lexus Ltd
with Dittoprint Ltd, Glasgow
Printed in Great Britain by Cambus Litho

First published in Great Britain in 1997
by Dorling Kindersley Limited
9 Henrietta Street, London WC2E 8PS

A CIP catalogue record is available from the British Library.
ISBN 0-7513-1075-1

CONTENTS

PREFACE

This *Eyewitness Travel Guide Phrase Book* has been compiled by experts to meet the general needs of tourists and business travellers. Arranged under the headings of Hotels, Motoring and so forth, the ample selection of useful words and phrases is supported by a 2,000-line mini-dictionary. There is also an extensive menu guide listing approximately 600 dishes or methods of cooking and presentation.

Typical replies to questions you may ask during your journey, and the signs or instructions you may see or hear, are shown in tinted boxes. In the main text, the pronunciation of Italian words and phrases is imitated in English sound syllables. The Introduction provides basic guidelines to Italian pronunciation, and lists some key grammatical points to remember.

Eyewitness Travel Guides are recognized as the world's best travel guides. Each title features specially commissioned colour photographs, cutaways of major buildings, 3-D aerial views and detailed maps, plus information on sights, events, hotels, restaurants, shopping and entertainment.

Titles available in the series are:
Italy • Rome • Venice & the Veneto • Florence & Tuscany
France • Paris • Provence • Loire Valley • London • Prague
New York • San Francisco • Sydney • California
Vienna • Amsterdam • Seville & Andalusia • Spain
The Greek Islands • Greece: Athens & the Mainland
Great Britain • Ireland

INTRODUCTION

PRONUNCIATION

When reading the imitated pronunciation, stress that part which is underlined. Pronounce each syllable as if it formed part of an English word, and you will be understood sufficiently well. Remember the points below, and your pronunciation will be even closer to the correct Italian. Use our audio-cassette of selected extracts from this book, and you should be word-perfect!

ai	as in 'fair'
ay	as in 'pay'
e	as in 'bed'
g	always hard as in 'get'
I	as in 'I'
ow	as in 'cow'
r	is always strongly pronounced
y	always pronounced as in 'yet' except in 'ay' as above

Note that when there are two identical consonants separated by a hyphen, eg **vorrei** – *vor-ray*, both consonants must be pronounced as if you were pronouncing two separate English words: eg **jus<u>t t</u>wo, fu<u>ll l</u>ength**.

GENDERS AND ARTICLES

Italian has two genders for nouns – masculine and feminine. In the vocabulary section of this book, we generally give the definite article ('the'). For masculine nouns, the definite article is **il** (plural **i**) before nouns beginning with a consonant; **lo** (plural **gli**) before nouns beginning with 's' + consonant or 'z'; and **l'** (plural **gli**) before nouns beginning with a vowel. For feminine nouns, use **la** before a noun beginning with a consonant and **l'** before a vowel (plural **le**).

The masculine indefinite article ('a') is **uno** before a noun beginning with a consonant and **un** before a vowel. The feminine is **una** before a consonant and **un'** before a vowel.

USEFUL EVERYDAY PHRASES

YES, NO, OK ETC

Yes/No
Sì/No
see/no

Excellent!
Ottimo!
ot-teemo

Don't!
Non farlo!
non farlo

OK
OK
'ok'

That's fine
Va bene
va baynay

That's right
È vero
eh vayro

GREETINGS, INTRODUCTIONS

How do you do, pleased to meet you
Piacere di conoscerla
pee-achairay dee konoshairla

Good morning/Good evening/Good night
Buon giorno/Buona sera/Buona notte
bwon jorno/bwona saira/bwona not-tay

Goodbye
Arrivederci
ar-reevedairchee

How are you?
Come sta?
komay sta

(familiar)
Come stai?
komay stɪ

My name is ...
Mi chiamo...
mee k-yamo

What's your name?
Come si chiama?
komay see k-yama

(familiar)
Come ti chiami?
komay tee k-yamee

What's his/her name?
Come si chiama?
komay see k-yama

May I introduce ...?
Posso presentarle...?
pos-so prezentarlay

This is ... *(introducing male/female)*
Questo è.../Questa è...
kwesto eh/kwesta eh

Hello
Ciao
chow

Hi!
Salve!
salvay

Bye!/Cheerio!
Ciao!
chow

7

See you later
A più tardi
a p-yoo tardee

It's been nice meeting you
Mi ha fatto piacere conoscerla
mee a fat-to pee-achairay konoshairla

PLEASE, THANK YOU, APOLOGIES

Thank you/No thank you
Grazie/No grazie
gratzee-ay/no gratzee-ay

Yes please
Sì grazie
see gratzee-ay

Please *(offering)*   *(asking for something)*
Prego   Per favore/per piacere
praygo   *pair favoray/pair pee-achairay*

Excuse me! *(when belching/sneezing etc)*
Scusate!
skoozatay

Sorry!   *(familiar)*
Scusi!   Scusa!
skoozee   *skooza*

I'm really sorry
Sono davvero spiacente
sono dav-vairo spee-achentay

It was/wasn't my fault!
È/non è stata colpa mia!
eh/non eh stata kolpa mee-a

WHERE, HOW, ASKING

Excuse me please *(to get past etc)*
Permesso
pairmesso

Can you tell me ...?
Potrebbe dirmi...?
potrayb-bay deermee

Can I have ...?
Potrei avere...?
potray avairay

Would you like a ...?
Vorrebbe un/una...?
vor-rayb-bay oon/oona

Would you like to ...?
Le piacerebbe...?
lay pee-achairayb-bay

Is there ... here?
C'è...?
cheh

What's that?
Che cos'è?
kay kozeh

Where can I get ...?
Dove potrei trovare...?
dovay potray trovaray

How much is it?
Quanto costa?
kwanto kosta

Where is the ...?
Dov'è il/la...?
dov<u>eh</u> eel/la

Where are the toilets, please?
Per cortesia, dove sono i servizi?
pair kortayz<u>ee</u>-a d<u>o</u>vay s<u>o</u>no ee sairv<u>ee</u>tzee

ABOUT ONESELF

I'm from ...
Sono di...
s<u>o</u>no dee

I'm ... years old
Ho... anni
oh ... <u>a</u>n-nee

I'm a ... *(occupation)*
Faccio il/la...
f<u>a</u>cho eel/la

I'm married/single/divorced *(said by a man)*
Sono sposato/celibe/divorziato
s<u>o</u>no spoz<u>a</u>to/ch<u>e</u>leebay/deevortz-y<u>a</u>to

(said by a woman)
Sono sposata/nubile/divorziata
s<u>o</u>no spoz<u>a</u>ta/n<u>oo</u>beelay/deevortz-y<u>a</u>ta

I have ... sisters/brothers/children
Ho... sorelle/fratelli/bambini
oh ... sor<u>e</u>l-lay/frat<u>e</u>l-lee/bamb<u>ee</u>nee

LIKES, DISLIKES, SOCIALIZING

I like/love ...
Mi piace...
mee pee-<u>a</u>chay

10

I don't like …
Non mi piace...
non mee pee-achay

I like swimming/travelling
Mi piace nuotare/viaggiare
mee pee-achay nwotaray/vyaj-jaray

I hate …
Odio...
odee-o

Do you like …?
Le piace...?
lay pee-achay

It's delicious/awful!
È buonissimo/terribile!
eh bwonees-seemo/ter-reebeelay

I don't drink/smoke
Non bevo/fumo
non bayvo/foomo

Do you mind if I smoke?
Le dispiace se fumo?
lay deespee-achay say foomo

I don't eat meat or fish
Non mangio nè la carne nè il pesce
non manjo neh la karnay neh eel peshay

What would you like (to drink)?
Cosa desidera (da bere)?
koza dezeedaira da bairay

I would like a …
Vorrei un/una...
vor-ray oon/oona

11

Nothing for me thanks
Per me niente, grazie
pair may nee-entay gratzee-ay

I'll get this one
Prenderò questo
prendairo kwesto

Cheers! *(toast)*
Alla salute!/Cin cin!
al-la salootay/cheen cheen

I would like to …
Vorrei...
vor-ray

Let's go to Florence/the cinema/the exhibition
Andiamo a Firenze/al cinema/alla mostra
and-yamo a feerentzay/al cheenema/al-la mostra

Let's go swimming/for a walk
Andiamo a nuotare/a fare una passeggiata
and-yamo a nwotaray/a faray oona pas-sej-jata

What's the weather like?
Che tempo fa?
kay tempo fa

The weather's awful
È brutto tempo
eh broot-to tempo

It's pouring down
Sta piovendo a dirotto
sta p-yovendo a deerot-to

It's really hot
Fa veramente caldo
fa veramentay kaldo

It's sunny
C'è il sole
cheh eel solay

HELP, PROBLEMS

Can you help me?
Può aiutarmi?
pwo i-ootarmee

I don't understand
Non capisco
non kapeesko

Do you speak English/French/German?
Parla inglese/francese/tedesco?
parla eenglayzay/franchayzay/tedesko

Does anyone here speak English?
C'è qualcuno che parla inglese?
cheh kwalkoono kay parla eenglayzay

I can't speak Italian
Non parlo italiano
non parlo eetal-yano

I don't know
Non so
non so

What's wrong?
Cosa c'è che non va?
koza cheh kay non va

Please speak more slowly
Per favore, parli più lentamente
pair favoray parlee p-yoo lentamentay

Please write it down for me
Me lo scriva, per favore
may lo skreeva pair favoray

I've lost my way *(said by a man/woman)*
Mi sono perso/persa
mee sono pairso/pairsa

Go away! *(familiar)*
Se ne vada! Vattene!
say nay vada *vat-tenay*

TALKING TO RECEPTIONISTS ETC

I have an appointment with ...
Ho un appuntamento con...
oh oon ap-poontamento kon

I'd like to see ...
Vorrei vedere...
vor-ray vedairay

Here's my card
Questo è il mio biglietto da visita
kwesto eh eel mee-o beel-yet-to da veez-eeta

My company is ...
La mia società è...
la mee-a socheta eh

May I use your phone?
Posso usare il telefono?
pos-so oozaray eel telefono

THINGS YOU'LL SEE

affittasi	to let
aperto	open

→

acqua potabile	drinking water
ascensore	lift
buffet	snack bar
cassa	till, cash point
chiuso	closed
chiuso per ferie	closed for holiday period
entrata	way in, entrance
entrata libera	admission free
feriali	working days
festivi	public holidays
gabinetti	toilets
libero	vacant, free
occupato	engaged
orario di apertura	opening hours
orario di visita	visiting hours
piano terra	ground floor
primo piano	first floor
riservato	reserved
saldi/sconti	sales
servizi	toilets
signore	ladies
signori	gents
si prega di non...	please do not ...
spingere	push
strada	road
svendita	sale
tirare	pull
ufficio informazioni	tourist information
uscita	exit, way out
uscita di sicurezza	emergency exit
vendesi	for sale
vernice fresca	wet paint
via	street
vietato	forbidden
vietato l'ingresso	no admittance

THINGS YOU'LL HEAR

a più tardi	see you later
arrivederci	goodbye
attenzione!	look out!, attention!
avanti!	come in!
bene	good, fine
buon viaggio!	have a good trip!
ciao!	hello!; cheerio!
come, scusi?	pardon?
come stai/sta/state?	how are you?
come va?	how are things?
cosa hai/ha detto?	what did you say?
davvero?	really?
ecco qua!	here you are!
esattamente	exactly
grazie	thanks
grazie, anche a lei	thank you, the same to you
grazie molte	thank you very much
mi dispiace tanto!	I'm so sorry!
mi scusi	excuse me
molto bene, grazie	very well, thank you
– e lei?	– and you?
non capisco	I don't understand
non so	I don't know
piacere di conoscerla	how do you do, nice to meet you
prego	you're welcome, don't mention it; please
prego?	pardon?
salve!	hi!
serviti/si serva/servitevi	help yourself
sì	yes
va bene	that's right

COLLOQUIALISMS

You may hear these: to use some of them yourself could be risky!

accidenti!	damn!
che schifo!	it's disgusting!
chiudi il becco!	shut up!
cretino	idiot, fool
Dio mio!	my God!
e allora?	so what?
è orribile!	it's awful!
fa' pure!	do as you please!, please, do!
grazie a Dio!	thank God!
maledetto...	cursed ...
maledizione!	damn!
ma va?	really?
ma va!	I don't believe it
meglio così	so much the better
merda!	shit!
muoviti!	hurry up!
non posso crederci!	I can't believe it!
occhio!	watch out!
per Dio!	by God!
porca miseria!	bloody hell!
prova!	just try!
sei pazzo?	you must be crazy!
sparisci!	scram!
stupendo!	brilliant!
svitato	cracked, nutty
ti sta bene!	it serves you right!
tizio	bloke
togliti dai piedi!	get out of the way!
va al diavolo!/va all'inferno!	go to hell!
va a quel paese!	get lost!
va bene!	that's fine!, it's OK!
zitto!	shut up!

DAYS, MONTHS, SEASONS

Sunday	domenica	*dom<u>e</u>neeka*
Monday	lunedì	*loonedee*
Tuesday	martedì	*martedee*
Wednesday	mercoledì	*mairkoledee*
Thursday	giovedì	*jovedee*
Friday	venerdì	*venairdee*
Saturday	sabato	*s<u>a</u>bato*

January	gennaio	*jen-n<u>a</u>-yo*
February	febbraio	*feb-br<u>a</u>-yo*
March	marzo	*m<u>a</u>rtzo*
April	aprile	*apr<u>ee</u>lay*
May	maggio	*m<u>a</u>j-jo*
June	giugno	*j<u>oo</u>n-yo*
July	luglio	*l<u>oo</u>l-yo*
August	agosto	*ag<u>o</u>sto*
September	settembre	*set-t<u>e</u>mbray*
October	ottobre	*ot-t<u>o</u>bray*
November	novembre	*nov<u>e</u>mbray*
December	dicembre	*deech<u>e</u>mbray*

Spring	primavera	*preemav<u>ai</u>ra*
Summer	estate	*est<u>a</u>tay*
Autumn	autunno	*owt<u>oo</u>n-no*
Winter	inverno	*eenv<u>ai</u>rno*

Christmas	Natale	*nat<u>a</u>lay*
Christmas Eve	la Vigilia di Natale	*veej<u>ee</u>l-ya dee nat<u>a</u>lay*
Good Friday	Venerdì Santo	*venaird<u>ee</u> s<u>a</u>nto*
Easter	Pasqua	*p<u>a</u>skwa*
New Year	Capodanno	*kapod<u>a</u>n-no*
New Year's Eve	San Silvestro	*san seelv<u>e</u>stro*
Whitsun	Pentecoste	*pentayk<u>o</u>stay*

NUMBERS

0 zero *tzairo*
1 uno *oono*
2 due *doo-ay*
3 tre *tray*
4 quattro *kwat-tro*
5 cinque *cheenkway*
6 sei *say*
7 sette *set-tay*
8 otto *ot-to*
9 nove *no-vay*

10 dieci *dee-aychee*
11 undici *oon-deechee*
12 dodici *doh-deechee*
13 tredici *tray-deechee*
14 quattordici *kwat-tor-deechee*
15 quindici *kween-deechee*
16 sedici *say-deechee*
17 diciassette *deechas-set-tay*
18 diciotto *deechot-to*
19 diciannove *deechan-no-vay*

20 venti *ventee*
21 ventuno *vent-oono*
22 ventidue *ventee-doo-ay*
30 trenta *trenta*
31 trentuno *trentoono*
32 trentadue *trentadoo-ay*
40 quaranta *kwaranta*
50 cinquanta *cheenkwanta*
60 sessanta *ses-santa*
70 settanta *set-tanta*
80 ottanta *ot-tanta*
90 novanta *novanta*
100 cento *chento*
110 centodieci *chento-dee-aychee*
200 duecento *doo-ay-chento*
1,000 mille *meelay*
10,000 diecimila *dee-aycheemeela*
20,000 ventimila *venteemeela*
50,000 cinquantamila *cheenkwantameela*
54,250 cinquantaquattromila duecentocinquanta *cheenkwanta-kwat-tro-meela doo-ay-chento-cheenkwanta*
100,000 centomila *chentomeela*
1,000,000 un milione *oon meel-yonay*

Note that thousands are written 1.000, 10.000 etc in Italian.

19

TIME

today	oggi	*oj-jee*
yesterday	ieri	*yairee*
tomorrow	domani	*domanee*
the day before yesterday	l'altro ieri	*laltro yairee*
the day after tomorrow	dopodomani	*dopodomanee*
this week	questa settimana	*kwesta set-teemana*
last week	la settimana scorsa	*set-teemana skorsa*
next week	la settimana prossima	*set-teemana pros-seema*
this morning	stamattina	*stamat-teena*
this afternoon	questo pomeriggio	*kwesto pomereej-jo*
this evening	stasera	*stasaira*
tonight	stanotte	*stanot-tay*
yesterday afternoon	ieri pomeriggio	*yairee pomereej-jo*
last night	ieri sera, ieri notte	*yairee saira, yairee not-tay*
tomorrow morning	domani mattina	*domanee mat-teena*
tomorrow night	domani sera	*domanee saira*
in three days	tra tre giorni	*tra tray jornee*
three days ago	tre giorni fa	*tray jornee fa*
late	tardi	*tardee*
early	presto	*presto*
soon	presto	*presto*
later on	più tardi	*p-yoo tardee*
at the moment	in questo momento	*een kwesto momento*
second	un secondo	*sekondo*
minute	un minuto	*meenooto*
two minutes	due minuti	*doo-ay meenootee*
quarter of an hour	un quarto d'ora	*kwarto dora*
half an hour	mezz'ora	*medzora*

three quarters of an hour	tre quarti d'ora	*tray kwartee dora*
hour	un'ora	*ora*
day	un giorno	*jorno*
week	una settimana	*set-teemana*
fortnight, two weeks	quindici giorni	*kween-deechee jornee*
month	un mese	*mayzay*
year	un anno	*an-no*
that day	quel giorno	*kwel jorno*
every day	ogni giorno	*on-yee jorno*
all day	tutto il giorno	*toot-to eel jorno*
the next day	il giorno dopo	*jorno dopo*

TELLING THE TIME

The hour is expressed in Italian by the ordinal number only: **sono le due** 'it's two o'clock'; 'at two o'clock' **alle due**. There is no equivalent of 'o'clock'. To say 'half past', add **e mezza** after the hour: **sono le due e mezza** 'it's half past two'. To say 'quarter past', add **e un quarto** 'and a quarter' to the hour: **sono le tre e un quarto** is 'it's a quarter past three'.

Quarter to the hour is expressed either by adding **e tre quarti** 'and three quarters' to the hour, or adding **meno un quarto** 'less a quarter' to the next hour. 'It's a quarter to eight' is therefore **sono le sette e tre quarti** OR **sono le otto meno un quarto**.

To express minutes past the hour, add the minutes to the hour: 'it's seven forty' **sono le sette e quaranta**. Minutes to the hour are expressed by adding **meno** followed by the number of minutes to the next hour: 'it's twenty to eight' **sono le otto meno venti**.

There are no equivalents of am and pm in Italian, although you could use **di mattina/del mattino** 'in the morning', **di/del pomeriggio** 'in the afternoon', **di sera** 'in the evening' and **di notte** 'at night'. For example: '10 am' **le dieci di mattina/del mattino**; '6 pm' **le sei di/del pomeriggio**; '10 pm' **le dieci di sera**; '2 am' **le due di notte** (but also **le due del mattino**)

The 24-hour clock is used much more frequently than in the

UK, both in the written form as in timetables, and verbally as in enquiry offices and when making appointments.

what time is it?	che ore sono?	*kay ǫray sono?*
it's one o'clock	è l'una	*eh lǫona*
it's two/three/four o'clock	sono le due/tre/ quattro	*sono lay dǫo-ay/tray/ kwǫt-tro*
ten past one	l'una e dieci	*lǫona ay dee-ǫychee*
quarter past one	l'una e un quarto	*lǫona ay oon kwǫrto*
half past one	l'una e mezza	*lǫona ay mędza*
twenty to two	le due meno venti	*lay dǫo-ay mǫyno ventee*
quarter to two	le due meno un quarto	*lay dǫo-ay mǫyno oon kwǫrto*
two o'clock	le due	*lay dǫo-ay*
13.00	le tredici	*lay trǫy-deechee*
16.30	le sedici e trenta	*lay sǫy-deechee ay trenta*
at half past five	alle cinque e mezza	*ǫl-lay cheenkway ay mędza*
at seven o'clock	alle sette	*ǫl-lay sęt-tay*
noon	mezzogiorno	*medzojorno*
midnight	mezzanotte	*medzanǫt-tay*

THE CALENDAR

The cardinal numbers on page 19 are used to express the date in Italian, except for the first when the ordinal **il primo** is used:

the first of May	il primo maggio	*eel pręemo mǫj-jo*
the second of September	il due settembre	*eel dǫo-ay set-tęmbray*
the twentieth of June	il venti giugno	*eel vęntee joǫn-yo*

HOTELS

Hotels in Italy are classified according to the familiar star system: one, two, three, four and five stars. At the bottom of the range you'll find **locande** (one-star hotels) and **pensioni** (one- or two-star hotels). The prices are displayed in the rooms and they do not always include breakfast, but should include service charges and taxes.

In some areas, the local **APT** (**Azienda di Promozione Turistica**) can supply information about hotels, but in others tourism is co-ordinated by an **AAST** (**Azienda Autonoma di Soggiorno e Turismo**). It is also possible to obtain a list of hotels from information offices in stations and airports. If you arrive in a town without having booked beforehand, go directly to the **APT** or to the **AAST** for help. Leaflets will be available in English and usually at least one person there will speak English.

Hotel breakfasts usually consist of a **brioche** (a type of croissant) or bread, butter and jam, and coffee or tea. Some hotels may provide an English breakfast on request.

USEFUL WORDS AND PHRASES

balcony	il balcone	*bal-k{o}nay*
bath *(tub)*	la vasca da bagno	*v{a}ska da b{a}n-yo*
bathroom	il bagno	*b{a}n-yo*
bed	il letto	*l{e}t-to*
bed and breakfast	camera con colazione	*k{a}maira kon kolatz-y{o}nay*
bed and breakfast hotel	la pensione familiare	*penz-y{o}nay fameel-y{a}ray*
bedroom	la camera da letto	*k{a}maira da l{e}t-to*
bill	il conto	*k{o}nto*
breakfast	la prima colazione	*pr{e}ema kolatz-y{o}nay*
car park	il parcheggio	*parkej-jo*
dining room	la sala da pranzo	*s{a}la da pr{a}ntzo*

dinner	la cena	*chayna*
double bed	il letto matrimoniale	*let-to matreemon-yalay*
double room	la stanza doppia	*stantza doppee-a*
foyer	la hall	*oll*
full board	la pensione completa	*pens-yonay komplayta*
guesthouse	la pensione,	*pens-yonay*
	la locanda	*lokanda*
half board	la mezza pensione	*medza pens-yonay*
hotel	l'albergo, l'hotel	*albairgo, oh-tel*
key	la chiave	*k-yavay*
lift	l'ascensore	*ashen-soray*
lounge	il salone	*salonay*
lunch	il pranzo,	*pranzo*
	la seconda colazione	*sekonda kolatz-yonay*
maid	la cameriera	*kamair-yaira*
manager	il direttore	*deeret-toray*
receipt	la ricevuta	*reechevoota*
reception	la reception	*'reception'*
receptionist	il/la receptionist	*'receptionist'*
restaurant	il ristorante	*reestorantay*
room	la camera, la stanza	*kamaira, stantza*
room service	il servizio in camera	*serveetz-yo een kamaira*
shower	la doccia	*docha*
single bed	il letto singolo	*let-to seengolo*
single room	la stanza singola	*stantza seengola*
toilet	la toilette	*twalet*
twin room	la stanza con due letti	*stantza kon doo-ay lettee*
washbasin	il lavabo	*lavabo*

Have you any vacancies?
Avete una stanza libera?
avaytay oona stantza leebaira

I have a reservation
Ho prenotato una stanza
oh praynotato oona stantza

I'd like a single room
Vorrei una stanza singola
vor-ray oona stantza seengola

I'd like a room with a bathroom/balcony
Vorrei una stanza con bagno/con il balcone
vor-ray oona stantza kon ban-yo/kon eel bal-konay

I'd like a room for one night/three nights
Vorrei una stanza per una notte/tre notti
vor-ray oona stantza pair oona not-tay/tray not-tee

What is the charge per night?
Quanto si paga per notte?
kwanto see paga pair not-tay

I don't know yet how long I'll stay
Non so ancora quanto tempo rimarrò
non so ankora kwanto tempo reemarro

When is breakfast/dinner?
A che ora viene servita la colazione/la cena?
a kay ora v-yaynay serveeta la kolatz-yonay/la chayna

Please wake me at 7 o'clock
Mi svegli, per favore, alle sette
mee zvel-yee pair favoray al-lay set-tay

Can I have breakfast in my room?
Potrei avere la colazione in camera?
potray avairay la kolatz-yonay een kamaira

I'd like to have some laundry done
Vorrei far pulire alcuni indumenti
vor-ray far pooleeray alkoonee eendoomentee

I'll be back at 10 o'clock
Tornerò alle dieci
tornairo al-lay dee-aychee

My room number is 205
Il mio numero di stanza è duecentocinque
eel mee-o noomero dee stantza eh doo-aychentocheenkway

My booking was for a double room
Avevo prenotato una stanza doppia
avayvo praynotato oona stantza dop-pia

I asked for a room with an en-suite bathroom
Avevo chiesto una stanza con bagno
avayvo k-yaysto oona stantza kon ban-yo

There is no toilet paper in the bathroom
Non c'è carta igienica in bagno
non cheh karta eej-yeneeka een ban-yo

The window won't open
La finestra non si apre
la feenestra non see apray

The lift/shower isn't working
L'ascensore/la doccia non funziona
lashen-soray/la docha non foontz-yona

There isn't any hot water
Non c'è acqua calda
non cheh akwa kalda

The socket in the bathroom doesn't work
La presa di corrente del bagno non funziona
la prayza dee kor-rentay del ban-yo non foontz-yona

I'm leaving tomorrow
Parto domani
parto domanee

When do I have to vacate the room?
Entro che ora devo liberare la camera?
entro kay ora dayvo leebairaray la kamaira

Can I have the bill please?
Mi da il conto per favore?
mee da eel konto pair favoray

I'll pay by credit card
Pago con la carta di credito
pago kon la karta dee kraydeeto

I'll pay cash
Pago in contanti
pago een kontantee

Can you get me a taxi?
Potrebbe chiamarmi un taxi per favore?
potrayb-bay k-yamarmee oon 'taxi' pair favoray

Can you recommend another hotel?
Potrebbe consigliarmi un altro albergo?
potrayb-bay konseel-yarmee oon altro albairgo

THINGS YOU'LL SEE

albergo	hotel
ascensore	lift
bagno	bathroom
camera con prima colazione	bed and breakfast
camera doppia	double room
camera singola	single room
cena	dinner
colazione	breakfast
completo	no vacancies
conto	bill
doccia	shower

→

27

entrata	entrance/way in
locanda	guesthouse
mezza pensione	half board
parcheggio	car park
parcheggio riservato agli ospiti dell'albergo	parking reserved for hotel patrons only
pensione	guesthouse
pensione completa	full board
pianterreno	ground floor
pranzo	lunch
prenotazione	reservation
primo piano	first floor
scale	stairs
seconda colazione	lunch
spingere	push
stanza con due letti	twin room
tirare	pull
uscita d'emergenza	emergency exit

REPLIES YOU MAY BE GIVEN

Mi spiace, siamo al completo
I'm sorry, we're full

Non ci sono più camere singole/doppie
There are no single/double rooms left

Per quante notti?
For how many nights?

Come vuole pagare?
How will you be paying?

Pagamento anticipato, per favore
Please pay in advance

Dovete liberare la stanza entro mezzogiorno
You must vacate the room by midday

CAMPING AND CARAVANNING

Campsites in Italy usually have excellent facilities. Prices differ according to the size of tent (**casetta** = 'little house'; **canadese** = 'two man tent'), and/or the number of people sharing it. You can generally pay for a parking space next to the tent. Moving the car at certain times, for example mealtimes, is forbidden as it raises dust. If you go out in the evening you will not be allowed to bring your car back inside the site after midnight, but there are often parking facilities just outside.

Most campsites have electricity generators, for the use of which a small daily fee will be added to your bill. Toilet and washing facilities are generally very good. You may have to pay for a hot shower with coins or tokens – which you insert into a machine attached to the shower. If tokens (**gettoni**) are needed these will be available at the campsite office. Cold showers are free. The campsite office usually acts as a mini-bank as well. You can deposit all your money there and withdraw it on a daily basis. The office will also exchange foreign currency.

USEFUL WORDS AND PHRASES

bonfire	il falò	_falo_
bucket	il secchio	_sek-yo_
go camping	andare in campeggio	_andaray een kampej-jo_
campsite	il campeggio	_kampej-jo_
caravan	la roulotte	_roolot_
caravan site	il campeggio	_kampej-jo_
cooking utensils	gli utensili da cucina	_ootenseelee da koocheena_
drinking water	l'acqua potabile	_akwa pota-beelay_
ground sheet	il telone impermeabile	_telonay eempair-may-abeelay_
hitchhike	fare l'autostop	_faray lowto-stop_
rope	la fune, la corda	_foonay, korda_

rubbish	l'immondizia	*eem-mondeetzee-a*
rucksack	lo zaino	*tza-eeno*
saucepans	le pentole	*pentolay*
sleeping bag	il sacco a pelo	*sak-ko a paylo*
tent	la tenda	*tenda*
tokens	i gettoni	*jet-tonee*
youth hostel	l'ostello della gioventù	*ostel-lo del-la joventoo*

Can I camp here?
Posso campeggiare qui?
pos-so kampej-jaray kwee

Can we park the caravan here?
Possiamo parcheggiare la roulotte qui?
poss-yamo parkej-jaray la roolot kwee

Where is the nearest campsite/caravan site?
Qual è il campeggio più vicino?
kwal eh eel kampej-jo p-yoo veecheeno

What is the charge per night?
Quanto si paga per notte?
kwanto see paga pair not-tay

I only want to stay for one night
Vorrei fermarmi solo una notte
vor-ray fairmarmee solo oona not-tay

How much is it for a week?
Quanto mi viene a costare per una settimana?
kwanto mee v-yaynay a kostaray pair oona set-teemana

We're leaving tomorrow
Partiamo domani
part-yamo domanee

Where is the kitchen?
Dov'è la cucina?
doveh la koocheena

Can I light a fire here?
Posso accendere il fuoco qui?
pos-so achendairay eel fwoko kwee

Can I have some tokens for the shower?
Potrei avere alcuni gettoni per la doccia?
potray avairay alkoonee jet-tonee pair la docha

Where can I get ...?
Dove posso trovare...?
dovay pos-so trovaray

Is there any drinking water?
C'è acqua potabile?
cheh akwa pota-beelay

THINGS YOU'LL SEE

acqua potabile	drinking water
a persona	per person
campeggio	campsite
cucina	kitchen
docce	showers
gabinetti	toilets
ostello della gioventù	youth hostel
rimorchio	trailer
roulotte	caravan, trailer
tariffa	charge
tenda	tent
vietato accendere fuochi	no campfires
vietato campeggiare	no camping

VILLAS AND APARTMENTS

In Italy you can arrange to rent a flat in travel agencies or from an estate agent. If you make a reservation, you will be asked to pay a deposit in advance.

When you arrive in the tourist resort where you reserved the villa or apartment, you will have to sign a contract. Your name, the date of rental, the address of the apartment, deposits, etc will be specified in this contract. You may be asked to pay for certain 'extras' not included in the original price (in particular tourist taxes). Gas and electricity are normally included, while cleaning seldom is. It's a good idea to ask about an inventory at the start, rather than be told something is missing later just as you are about to leave; sometimes you will find an inventory in the apartment (in a drawer or in a cupboard). Usually, you are not required to sign it.

You may be asked for a deposit, in case you break something. Make sure this is specified in the contract you signed. You will get your money back when you leave.

USEFUL WORDS AND PHRASES

bath *(tub)*	la vasca da bagno	*vaska da ban-yo*
bathroom	il bagno	*ban-yo*
bedroom	la camera da letto	*kamaira da let-to*
blocked	intasato	*eentazato*
boiler	lo scaldabagno	*skaldaban-yo*
broken	rotto	*rot-to*
caretaker	il portinaio	*porteenι-o*
(female)	la portinaia	*porteenι-a*
central	il riscaldamento	*reeskaldamento*
heating	centrale	*chentralay*
cleaner	l'uomo delle pulizie	*womo del-lay pooleetzee-ay*
(female)	la donna delle pulizie	*don-na del-lay pooleetzee-ay*

32

cooker	il fornello	*fornel-lo*
deposit *(security)*	la cauzione	*kowtz-yonay*
(part payment)	la caparra	*kapar-ra*
drain	lo scarico	*skareeko*
dustbin	il bidone della spazzatura	*beedonay del-la spatz-zatoora*
duvet	il piumino	*p-yoomeeno*
electrician	l'elettricista	*elet-treecheesta*
electricity	l'elettricità	*elet-treecheeta*
estate agent	l'agente immobiliare	*ajentay eem-mobeelyaray*
fridge	il frigorifero	*freegoreefairo*
fusebox	la scatola dei fusibili	*skatola day foozeebeelee*
gas	il gas	*'gas'*
grill	la griglia	*greel-ya*
heater	il calorifero	*kaloreefairo*
iron	il ferro da stiro	*fair-ro da steero*
ironing board	la tavola da stiro	*tavola da steero*
keys	le chiavi	*k-ya-vee*
kitchen	la cucina	*koocheena*
leak *(noun)*	la perdita	*pairdeeta*
(verb)	perdere	*pairdairay*
light	la luce	*loochay*
living room	il soggiorno	*soj-jorno*
maid	la cameriera	*kamair-yaira*
pillow	il cuscino	*koosheeno*
pillow slip	la federa	*fedaira*
plumber	l'idraulico	*eedrowleeko*
refund	il rimborso	*reemborso*
sheets	le lenzuola	*lentzwola*
shower	la doccia	*docha*
sink	il lavandino	*lavandeeno*
stopcock	il rubinetto d'arresto	*roobeenet-to dar-resto*
swimming pool	la piscina	*peesheena*
tap	il rubinetto	*roobeenet-to*
toilet	il gabinetto	*gabeenet-to*

towel	l'asciugamano	*ashoogam<u>a</u>no*
washing machine	la lavatrice	*lavatr<u>ee</u>chay*
water	l'acqua	*<u>a</u>kwa*
water heater	lo scaldaacqua	*skalda-<u>a</u>kwa*

I'd like to rent an apartment/villa for … days
Vorrei affittare un appartamento/una villa per… giorni
vor-r<u>ay</u> af-feet-t<u>a</u>ray oon ap-partam<u>e</u>nto/<u>oo</u>na v<u>ee</u>l-la pair … j<u>o</u>rnee

Do I have to pay a deposit?
Devo versare una cauzione?
d<u>a</u>yvo vairs<u>a</u>ray <u>oo</u>na kowtz-y<u>o</u>nay

Does the price include gas and electricity?
Il gas e l'elettricità sono inclusi nel prezzo?
eel 'gas' ay lelet-treecheet<u>a</u> s<u>o</u>no eenkl<u>oo</u>zee nel pr<u>e</u>tzo

Where is this item?
Dove si trova questo oggetto?
d<u>o</u>vay see tr<u>o</u>va kw<u>e</u>sto oj-j<u>e</u>t-to

Please take it off the inventory
Lo tolga dall'inventario, per favore
lo t<u>o</u>lga dal-leenvent<u>a</u>r-yo pair fav<u>o</u>ray

We've broken this
Abbiamo rotto questo
abb-y<u>a</u>mo r<u>o</u>t-to kw<u>e</u>sto

This was broken when we arrived
Era già rotto quando siamo arrivati
<u>a</u>yra j<u>a</u> r<u>o</u>t-to kw<u>a</u>ndo s-y<u>a</u>mo ar-reev<u>a</u>tee

This was missing when we arrived
Non c'era quando siamo arrivati
non ch<u>a</u>yra kw<u>a</u>ndo s-y<u>a</u>mo ar-reev<u>a</u>tee

Can I have my deposit back?
Potrei riavere la cauzione?
potray ree-avairay la kowtz-yonay

Can we have an extra bed?
Potremmo avere un letto in più?
potraym-mo avairay oon let-to een p-yoo

Can we have more crockery/cutlery?
Potremmo avere ancora un po' di stoviglie/posate?
potraym-mo avairay ankora oon po dee stoveel-yay/pozatay

When does the maid come?
Quando viene la cameriera?
kwando v-yaynay la kamair-yaira

Where can I buy/find ...?
Dove posso comprare/trovare...?
dovay pos-so kompraray/trovaray

How does the water heater work?
Come funziona lo scaldaacqua?
komay foontz-yona lo skalda-akwa

Do you do ironing/baby-sitting?
Sa stirare/badare ai bambini?
sa steeraray/badaray i bambeenee

Do you prepare lunch/dinner?
È in grado di preparare il pranzo/la cena?
eh een grado dee praypararay eel prantzo/la chayna

Do we have to pay extra or is it included?
Dobbiamo pagarlo a parte o è incluso nel prezzo?
dobb-yamo pagarlo a partay oh eh eenkloozo nel pret-zo

The shower doesn't work
La doccia non funziona
la docha non foontz-yona

The sink is blocked
Il lavandino è intasato
eel lavandeeno eh eentazato

The sink/toilet is leaking
Il lavandino/gabinetto perde
eel lavandeeno/gabeenet-to pairday

There's a burst pipe
Si è rotto un tubo
see eh rot-to oon toobo

The rubbish has not been collected for a week
Non portano via la spazzatura da una settimana
non portano vee-a la spatz-zatoora da oona set-teemana

There's no electricity/gas/water
Non c'è elettricità/gas/acqua
non cheh elet-treecheeta/'gas'/akwa

Can you mend it today?
Può ripararlo oggi?
pwo reepararlo oj-jee

Send your bill to …
Mandi il conto a...
mandee eel konto a

I'm staying at …
Sto a...
sto a

Thank you for everything!
Grazie di tutto!
gratzee-ay dee toot-to

See you again next year!
Al prossimo anno!
al pros-seemo an-no

MOTORING

In Italy you drive on the right and overtake on the left. On dual carriageways you may stay in the left-hand lane if heavy traffic has taken over the right-hand lane. Normally you may move from the right to the left-hand lane only for turning or overtaking. On three-lane roads with traffic flowing in both directions the central lane is for overtaking only.

At junctions where there are no indications or traffic lights, you must give way to traffic coming from the right, except in the case of a service station exit, a private road or a track entering the main road. Usually, a diamond-shaped yellow sign tells you that you have right of way; the end of this right of way is indicated by a similar sign with a bar through it. An upside-down red triangle or a 'STOP' sign indicates that you must give way to all vehicles coming both from the right and from the left.

In built-up areas the speed limit is 50km/h (31 mph). On open roads (if not otherwise indicated) it is 90km/h (56 mph) and on motorways it is 130 km/h (81 mph).

If you break down and are forced to stop in the middle of the road, you must place a red triangle 50 metres behind your vehicle to warn other drivers. All drivers must carry this triangle – which can be rented from the offices of the **ACI** (**Automobile Club Italiano**) on entering Italy and then returned on leaving the country.

There are emergency telephones on most motorways. If you break down on the **Autostrada del Sole** (Milan-Rome) or on another main motorway there are emergency telephones on the right side of the motorway at intervals of 1 or 2 kms. Generally, it is illegal to walk along the motorway or hitchhike, but if the breakdown occurs between two telephones, you are allowed to walk to the next emergency telephone. (See also EMERGENCIES page 107.)

Most town centres are pedestrian precincts, and if you park where you are not supposed to, your car will be towed away. You should park either in a free parking area or in a paying car park or

garage. Charges are displayed on a notice board in the car park.
You'll be given a parking ticket when you arrive, or, if there is a
car-park attendant, he will place a ticket on your windscreen and
you pay on departure.

SOME COMMON ROAD SIGNS

accendere i fari	headlights on
attenzione	watch out, caution
autostrada	motorway (with toll)
banchina non transitabile	soft verge
caduta massi	falling rocks
centro	town centre
code	traffic queues ahead
controllo automatico della velocità	automatic speed monitor
cunetta o dosso	ditch
deviazione	diversion
disporsi su due file	two-lane traffic
divieto di accesso	no entry
divieto di fermata	no stopping
divieto di transito	no thoroughfare
dogana	customs
escluso frontisti	residents only
fine del tratto autostradale	end of motorway
ghiaccio	ice
incrocio	junction
incrocio pericoloso	dangerous junction/crossroads
informazioni turistiche	tourist information
lavori in corso	roadworks
nebbia	fog
non oltrepassare	no trespassing
pagare qui	pay here
parcheggio a giorni alterni	parking on alternate days
parcheggio a pagamento	paying car-park

→

parcheggio custodito	car park with attendant
parcheggio incustodito	unattended car park
pedaggio	toll
pedoni	pedestrians
pericolo	danger
pista ciclabile	cycle track
provinciale	main road
rallentare	reduce speed
scuola	school
senso unico	one way
sosta vietata	no parking
sottopassaggio	subway
strada a fondo cieco	blind alley
strada camionabile	route for heavy vehicles
strada ghiacciata	ice on road
strada provinciale	main road
strada sdrucciolevole	slippery road
strada secondaria	secondary road
strada statale	main road
superstrada	motorway
uscita camion	works exit
veicoli lenti	crawler lane
zona a traffico limitato	restricted traffic area
zona pedonale	pedestrian precinct

USEFUL WORDS AND PHRASES

automatic	con il cambio automatico	*kon eel kam-bee-o owtomateeko*
bonnet	il cofano	*kofano*
boot	il portabagagli	*portabagal-yee*
brake	il freno	*frayno*
breakdown	il guasto	*gwasto*
car	l'automobile, la macchina	*owtomobeelay, mak-keena*

caravan	la roulotte	*roolot*
car ferry	il traghetto	*traget-to*
car park	il parcheggio	*parkej-jo*
clutch	la frizione	*freetz-yonay*
crossroads	l'incrocio	*eenkrocho*
drive	guidare	*gweedaray*
engine	il motore	*motoray*
exhaust	lo scappamento	*skap-pamento*
fanbelt	la cinghia della ventola	*cheeng-ya del-la ventola*
garage *(repairs)*	l'autorimessa	*owtoreemes-sa*
(for petrol)	la stazione di servizio	*statz-yonay dee sairveetz-yo*
gear	il cambio	*kam-bee-o*
gear box	la scatola del cambio	*skatola del kam-bee-o*
gears	le marce	*marchay*
headlights	i fari	*faree*
indicator	l'indicatore di direzione,	*eendeekatoray dee deeretz-yonay,*
	la freccia	*frech-cha*
junction	l'incrocio	*eenkrocho*
(motorway entry)	raccordo di entrata	*rak-kordo dee entrata*
(motorway exit)	raccordo di uscita	*rak-kordo dee oosheeta*
licence	la patente	*patentay*
lorry	il camion,	*kam-yon,*
	l'autocarro	*owtokar-ro*
manual	con il cambio manuale	*kon eel kam-bee-o manwalay*
mirror	lo specchietto	*spekk-yet-to*
motorbike	la motocicletta	*motocheeklet-ta*
motorway	l'autostrada	*owtostrada*
number plate	la targa	*targa*
petrol	la benzina	*bendzeena*
petrol station	la stazione di servizio	*statz-yonay dee sairveetz-yo*
rear lights	i fari posteriori	*faree postair-yoree*
road	la strada	*strada*

spares	i pezzi di ricambio	_petzee dee reekam-bee-o_
spark plug	la candela	_kandayla_
speed	la velocità	_velocheeta_
speed limit	il limite di velocità	_leemeetay dee velocheeta_
speedometer	il tachimetro	_takeemetro_
steering wheel	il volante	_volantay_
traffic lights	il semaforo	_semaforo_
trailer	il rimorchio	_reemork-yo_
tyre	la gomma	_gom-ma_
van	il furgone	_foorgonay_
warning triangle	il triangolo	_tree-angolo_
wheel	la ruota	_rwota_
windscreen	il parabrezza	_parabretza_
windscreen wiper	il tergicristallo	_tairjee-kreestal-lo_

Could you check the oil/water level, please?
Potrebbe controllare il livello dell'olio/dell'acqua, per favore?
potrayb-bay kontrol-laray eel leevel-lo del ol-yo/del akwa pair favoray

Fill her up please!
Faccia il pieno, per cortesia!
facha eel p-yayno pair kortayzee-a

I'd like 35 litres of 4-star
Mi dia trentacinque litri di super, per favore
mee dee-a trentacheenkway leetree dee soopair pair favoray

Do you do repairs?
Effettua riparazioni?
ef-fet-too-a reeparatz-yonee

Can you repair the clutch?
Può ripararmi la frizione?
pwo reepararmee la freetz-yonay

There is something wrong with the engine
C'è qualcosa che non va nel motore
cheh kwalkoza kay non va nel motoray

41

The engine is overheating
Il motore si surriscalda
eel motoray see soor-reeskalda

I need a new tyre
Ho bisogno di una gomma nuova
oh beezon-yo dee oona gom-ma nwova

Can you replace this?
Può sostituirlo?
pwo sosteetoo-eerlo

The indicator is not working
La freccia non funziona
la frech-cha non foontz-yona

How long will it take?
Quanto tempo ci vorrà?
kwanto tempo chee vor-ra

Where can I park?
Dove posso parcheggiare?
dovay pos-so parkej-jaray

I'd like to hire a car
Vorrei noleggiare una macchina
vor-ray nolej-jaray oona mak-keena

I'd like an automatic/a manual
Vorrei una macchina con il cambio automatico/manuale
vor-ray oona mak-keena kon eel kam-bee-o owtomateeko/ manwalay

How much is it for one day?
Quanto costa per un giorno?
kwanto kosta pair oon jorno

Is there a mileage charge?
C'è un supplemento per il chilometraggio?
cheh oon soop-plemento pair eel keelometraj-jo

When do I have to return it?
Quando devo riportarla?
kwando dayvo reeportarla

Where is the nearest petrol station?
Dov'è la stazione di servizio più vicina?
doveh la statz-yonay dee sairveetz-yo p-yoo veecheena

How do I get to ...?
Può dirmi come andare a...?
pwo deermee komay andaray a

Is this the road to ...?
È questa la strada per...?
eh kwesta la strada pair

Which is the quickest way to ...?
Qual è la strada più breve per...?
kwal eh la strada p-yoo brayvay pair

DIRECTIONS YOU MAY BE GIVEN

a destra	right
a sinistra	left
dritto	straight on
giri a destra	turn right
giri a sinistra	turn left
il primo/la prima a destra	first on the right
il secondo/la seconda a sinistra	second on the left
vada oltre...	go past the ...

THINGS YOU'LL SEE

acqua	water
area di servizio	service area

→

43

aspirapolvere	vacuum cleaner
autolavaggio	car wash
autorimessa	garage (for repairs)
benzina	petrol
benzina normale	two- or three-star petrol
benzina senza piombo	unleaded petrol
benzina super	four-star petrol
casello autostradale	motorway toll booth
cera per auto	car wax
code	traffic queue
deviazione	diversion
gasolio	diesel oil
gommista	tyre repairs
guidare a passo d'uomo	drive at walking speed
liquido tergicristallo	screen wash
olio	oil
raccordo autostradale	motorway junction
spegnere il motore	switch off engine
spingere	push
stazione di servizio	service station
uscita	exit
tirare	pull
vietato fumare	no smoking

THINGS YOU'LL HEAR

Vuole una macchina con il cambio automatico o manuale?
Would you like an automatic or a manual?

Esibisca la patente, per favore
May I see your licence, please?

Mi fa vedere il passaporto, per favore?
May I see your passport, please?

TRAVELLING AROUND

RAIL TRAVEL

Rail travel is so cheap in Italy that it is very widely used. During the tourist season travelling by train can be difficult so, wherever possible, you should book your seat well in advance. Children under four years of age not occupying a seat travel free, and there is a half-price fare for children aged between four and twelve years. Considerable reductions are available for families and individuals on short-term season tickets. Couchettes are available on most domestic long-distance night services and most long-distance trains have restaurant cars. On shorter journeys there will be a trolley on the train from which you can buy sandwiches and soft drinks. In main stations, platform vendors pass by the train windows.

Trains on Italian State Railways (**Ferrovie dello Stato** or **FS**) are classified as follows:

EC (Eurocity): very fast international train, with first and second class compartments. A supplement must be paid in advance but there is no charge for booking a seat in advance.

IC (Intercity): very fast national train. Most **IC**s have first and second class, but there are still a few of them with first class only. It's best to check this before departure. A supplement must be paid in advance but reserving a seat is free.

Espresso: long-distance fast train. No supplement required.

Diretto: long-distance train stopping at main stations.

Regionale: small local train stopping at nearly every station.

You should find out in advance whether you will be taking an **IC** or **EC** train and ask to pay the supplement when you buy your ticket. If you have a return ticket, you should validate the return journey by stamping the date on it on the day you return. In most stations, there are ticket-stamping machines but, in small stations, you should go to the ticket office.

LONG-DISTANCE BUS TRAVEL

People rarely travel long distances by coach in Italy as the rail service is so cheap and travelling by train is quicker. Local coaches for small towns and places of interest are generally inexpensive and the service frequent. The coaches often have a system similar to that of local buses: when you enter you stamp your ticket in the ticket-stamping machine.

LOCAL PUBLIC TRANSPORT

In large cities there are several types of public transport: bus, trolley bus (**filobus**), tram and underground (**Metropolitana**). In some cities there is an integrated public transport system, which means that the same tickets can be used on all types of transport. Tickets are cheap and operate on a flat-fare basis. In most cities, they are valid for 60 to 75 minutes but in some they are only valid for a one-way trip. Tickets can be bought in the underground, at any newspaper kiosk, **tabaccaio** or ordinary bar with a '**vendita biglietti**' sign in the window. When you enter a bus, **filobus** etc, you must insert your ticket into a machine which stamps the time on it. The only restriction on use of the ticket is that you cannot re-enter the **Metropolitana** with the same ticket, even if you have not yet used up your 75 minutes. There are inspectors who make random checks, and if you are travelling without a valid ticket you can expect an on-the-spot fine of about 20,000 lire. In most places public transport is very quick and efficient. Smoking is forbidden on all local public transport.

TAXI AND BOAT

It is advisable not to travel in a taxi which does not have the 'taxi' sign on top. Taxis without this sign are private taxis and may charge astronomical prices. The marked taxis are reliable and efficient but they do have a high minimum charge. Moreover, there is always an extra charge for each item of luggage and for journeys undertaken at night.

In Venice (where of course there are no buses etc) you travel by **vaporetto**, a small passenger boat. You must buy your ticket in advance from the kiosk at **vaporetti** stops. There is a flat fare for all destinations. There are, however, special offers, such as cheap 24-hour tickets with which you can travel on any number of boats for any distance, starting from the time when you stamp your ticket at the boat stop (not from when you buy it).

USEFUL WORDS AND PHRASES

airport	l'aeroporto	*a-airoporto*
airport bus	l'autobus per l'aeroporto	*owtoboos pair la-airoporto*
aisle seat	il posto vicino al corridoio	*posto veecheeno al kor-reedo-yo*
adult	l'adulto	*adoolto*
baggage claim	il ritiro bagagli	*reeteero bagal-yee*
boarding card	la carta d'imbarco	*karta deembarko*
boat	la barca, il battello	*barka, bat-taylo*
booking office	la biglietteria	*beel-yet-teree-a*
buffet	il buffet	*boofay*
bus	l'autobus	*owtoboos*
bus station	la stazione degli autobus	*statz-yonay del-yee owtoboos*
bus stop	la fermata dell'autobus	*fermata del lowtoboos*
check-in desk	l'accettazione (bagagli)	*achet-tatz-yonay bagal-yee*
child	il bambino	*bambeeno*
(female)	la bambina	*bambeena*
coach *(bus)*	la corriera	*kor-ree-aira*
compartment	lo scompartimento	*skomparteemento*
connection	la coincidenza	*ko-eencheedentza*
couchette	la cuccetta	*kooch-chet-ta*
cruise	la crociera	*krochaira*
customs	la dogana	*dogana*

departure lounge	la sala d'attesa	*sala dat-tayza*
domestic	nazionale	*natz-yonalay*
emergency exit	l'uscita di sicurezza	*oosheeta dee seekooretza*
entrance	l'entrata	*entrata*
exit	l'uscita	*oosheeta*
fare	la tariffa	*tareef-fa*
ferry	il traghetto	*trag-et-to*
first class	la prima classe	*preema klas-say*
flight	il volo	*volo*
flight number	il numero del volo	*noomairo del volo*
gate	l'uscita	*oosheeta*
hand luggage	il bagaglio a mano	*bagal-yo a mano*
international	internazionale	*eentairnatz-yonalay*
left luggage office	il deposito bagagli	*depozeeto bagal-yee*
lost property office	l'ufficio oggetti smarriti	*oof-feecho ojet-tee zmar-reetee*
luggage trolley	il carrello	*kar-rel-lo*
network map	la piantina dei trasporti pubblici	*p-yanteena day trasportee poob-bleechee*
non-smoking	non fumatori	*non foomatoree*
number 5 bus	l'autobus numero cinque	*owtoboos noomayro cheenkway*
passport	il passaporto	*pas-saporto*
platform	il binario	*beenaree-o*
railway	la ferrovia	*fer-rovee-a*
reserved seat	il posto riservato	*posto ree-sairvato*
restaurant car	il vagone ristorante	*vagonay reestorantay*
return ticket	il biglietto di andata e ritorno	*beel-yet-to dee andata ay reetorno*
seat	il posto	*posto*
second class	la seconda classe	*sekonda klas-say*
single ticket	la biglietto di sola andata	*beel-yet-to dee sola andata*
sleeper	il vagone letto	*vagonay let-to*
smoking	fumatori	*foomatoree*
station	la stazione	*statz-yonay*

subway	il sottopassaggio	*sot-topas-saj-jo*
taxi	il taxi	*'taxi'*
terminus	il capolinea	*kapoleenay-a*
ticket	il biglietto	*beel-yet-to*
timetable	l'orario	*orar-yo*
train	il treno	*trayno*
tram	il tram	*'tram'*
trolley bus	il filobus	*feeloboos*
underground	la metropolitana	*metro-poleetana*
waiting room	la sala d'attesa	*sala dat-tayza*
window seat	il posto vicino al finestrino	*posto veecheeno al feenestreeno*

AIR TRAVEL

I'd like a non-smoking seat please
Vorrei un posto per non fumatori, per favore
vor-ray oon posto pair non foomatoree pair favoray

I'd like a window seat please
Vorrei un posto vicino al finestrino
vor-ray oon posto veecheeno al feenestreeno

How long will the flight be delayed?
Con quanto ritardo partirà il volo?
kon kwanto reetardo parteera eel volo

Which gate for the flight to London?
Qual è l'uscita del volo per Londra?
kwal eh loosheeta del volo pair londra

RAIL AND BUS TRAVEL

When does the train/bus for Florence leave?
A che ora parte il treno/l'autobus per Firenze?
a kay ora partay eel trayno/lowtoboos pair feerentzay

49

When does the train/bus from Rome arrive?
A che ora arriva il treno/l'autobus da Roma?
a kay ora ar-reeva eel trayno/lowtoboos da roma

When is the next train/bus to Venice?
A che ora c'è il prossimo treno/autobus per Venezia?
a kay ora cheh eel pros-seemo trayno/owtoboos pair venetzee-a

When is the first/last train/bus to Turin?
A che ora c'è il primo/l'ultimo treno/autobus per Torino?
a kay ora cheh eel preemo/loolteemo trayno/owtoboos pair toreeno

What is the fare to Naples?
Quanto costa il biglietto per Napoli?
kwanto kosta eel beel-yet-to pair napolee

Do I have to change?
Devo cambiare?
dayvo kamb-yaray

Does the train/bus stop at Padua?
Il treno/l'autobus ferma a Padova?
eel trayno/lowtoboos fairma a padova

How long does it take to get to Trieste?
Quanto tempo ci s'impiega per andare a Trieste?
kwanto tempo chee seemp-yayga pair andaray a tree-estay

Where can I buy a ticket?
Dove posso comprare il biglietto?
dovay pos-so kompraray eel beel-yet-to

A single/return ticket to Bologna please
Un biglietto di sola andata/di andata e ritorno per Bologna, per favore
oon beel-yet-to dee sola andata/dee andata ay reetorno pair bolon-ya pair favoray

Could you help me get a ticket?
Potrebbe aiutarmi a prendere il biglietto?
potrayb-bay i-ootarmee a prendairay eel beel-yet-to

Do I have to pay a supplement?
Devo pagare un supplemento?
dayvo pagaray oon soop-plemento

I'd like to reserve a seat
Vorrei prenotare un posto a sedere
vor-ray praynotaray oon posto a sedayray

REPLIES YOU MAY BE GIVEN

Il prossimo treno parte alle diciotto
The next train leaves at 18.00 hours

Deve cambiare a Firenze
Change at Florence

Deve pagare un supplemento
You must pay a supplement

Non ci sono più posti per Catania
There are no more seats available for Catania

Is this the right train/bus for Genoa?
È questo il treno/l'autobus per Genova?
eh kwesto eel trayno/lowtoboos pair jenova

Is this the right platform for the Palermo train?
È questo il binario del treno per Palermo?
eh kwesto eel beenaree-o del trayno pair palairmo

Which platform for the Perugia train?
A che binario parte il treno per Perugia?
a kay beenaree-o partay eel trayno pair perooja

Is the train/bus late?
Il treno/l'autobus è in ritardo?
eel trayno/lowtoboos eh een reetardo

51

Could you help me with my luggage please?
Potrebbe darmi una mano con i bagagli, per favore?
potrayb-bay darmee oona mano kon ee bagal-yee pair favoray

Is this a non-smoking compartment?
È uno scompartimento non fumatori?
eh oono skomparteemento non foomatoree

Is this seat free?
È libero questo posto?
eh leebairo kwesto posto

This seat is taken
Questo posto è occupato
kwesto posto eh ok-koopato

I have reserved this seat
Questo posto è riservato
kwesto posto eh ree-sairvato

May I open/close the window?
Posso aprire/chiudere il finestrino?
pos-so apreeray/k-yoodairay eel feenestreeno

When do we arrive in Bari?
A che ora arriviamo a Bari?
a kay ora arreev-yamo a baree

What station is this?
Che stazione è questa?
kay statz-yonay eh kwesta

Do we stop at Pisa?
Ci fermiamo a Pisa?
chee fairmee-amo a peeza

Would you keep an eye on my things for a moment?
Le dispiace dare un'occhiata alla mia roba per un momento?
*lay deespee-achay daray oon okk-yata al-la mee-a roba pair oon
momento*

Is there a restaurant car on this train?
C'è un vagone ristorante su questo treno?
cheh oon vagonay reestorantay soo kwesto trayno

LOCAL PUBLIC TRANSPORT

Where is the nearest underground station?
Qual è la stazione della metropolitana più vicina?
kwal eh la statz-yonay del-la metro-poleetana p-yoo veecheena

Where is the bus station?
Dov'è la stazione degli autobus?
doveh la statz-yonay del-yee owtoboos

Which buses go to Mantua?
Quale autobus va a Mantova?
kwalay owtoboos va a mantova

How often do the buses to San Gimignano run?
Ogni quanto passa l'autobus per San Gimignano?
on-yee kwanto pas-sa lowtoboos pair san jeemeen-yano

Will you let me know when we're there?
Mi potrebbe avvertire quando arriviamo là?
mee potrayb-bay av-verteeray kwando ar-reev-yamo la

Do I have to get off yet?
Devo scendere qui?
dayvo shendairay kwee

How do you get to Asti?
Come posso andare ad Asti?
komay pos-so andaray ad astee

I want to go to Udine
Voglio andare a Udine
vol-yo andaray a oodeenay

Do you go near Enna?
Passa vicino ad Enna?
p<u>a</u>s-sa veech<u>ee</u>no ad <u>e</u>n-na

TAXI AND BOAT

To the airport please
All'aeroporto, per favore
alla-airop<u>o</u>rto pair fav<u>o</u>ray

How much will it cost?
Quanto mi verrà a costare?
kw<u>a</u>nto mee vair-r<u>a</u> a kost<u>a</u>ray

Please stop here
Si fermi qui, per favore
see f<u>ai</u>rmee kwee pair fav<u>o</u>ray

Could you wait here for me and take me back?
Può aspettarmi qui per riportarmi indietro?
pwo aspet-t<u>a</u>rmee kwee pair reeport<u>a</u>rmee eend-y<u>ay</u>tro

Where can I get the boat to Sirmione?
Dove posso prendere il battello per Sirmione?
d<u>o</u>vay p<u>o</u>s-so pr<u>e</u>ndairay eel bat-t<u>e</u>llo pair seerm-y<u>o</u>nay

---

THINGS YOU'LL SEE

abbonamento mensile	monthly ticket
abbonamento settimanale	weekly ticket
ai binari/treni	to the platforms/trains
arrivi	arrivals
bambini	children
biglietto	ticket
biglietto d'accesso ai treni	platform ticket
biglietto giornaliero	day ticket
biglietto valido per più corse	multi-journey ticket

cambiare	to change
cambio	bureau de change
capolinea	terminus
carrozza	carriage, car
controllo bagagli	baggage control
controllo biglietti	ticket inspection
controllo passaporti	passport control
cuccetta	sleeper
deposito bagagli	left luggage
diretto	long-distance train
discesa	exit
distributore automatico di biglietti	ticket machine
entrata	way in, entrance
è pericoloso sporgersi	it is dangerous to lean out
espresso	long-distance fast train
fermata	stop
Ferrovie dello Stato/FS	State Railways
fumatori	smokers
giro in barca	boat trip
informazioni	information
la domenica	Sundays
la domenica e i giorni festivi	Sundays and public holidays
libero	free
macchina obliteratrice	ticket-stamping machine
nazionale	domestic
non ferma a...	does not stop at ...
non fumatori	non-smokers
non parlare al conducente	do not speak to the driver
occupato	engaged, reserved
oggetti smarriti	lost property
ogni abuso sarà punito con...	penalty for misuse ...
ora locale	local time
orario	timetable
orario di volo	flight time
percorso	route

→

partenze	departures
passeggeri	passengers
porto	harbour, port
posti in piedi	standing room
posto (a sedere)	seat
posto prenotato	reserved seat
rapido	fast train
riservato ai non fumatori	non-smokers only
ritardo	delay
ritiro bagagli	baggage claim
sala d'attesa	waiting room
salita	entry
(segnale d')allarme	emergency alarm
solo il sabato/la domenica	Saturdays/Sundays only
spuntini, panini	snacks, sandwiches
supplemento rapido	supplement for fast train
tesserino	travel card
tragitto breve	short journey
uscita	exit
uscita di sicurezza	emergency exit
vagone	carriage, car
vagone letto	sleeper
vagone ristorante	restaurant car
viaggio	journey
vietato fumare	no smoking
vietato l'ingresso	no entry
vietato sporgersi	do not lean out
volo	flight
volo di linea	scheduled flight

THINGS YOU'LL HEAR

Ha bagagli?
Have you any luggage?

→

Fumatori o non fumatori?
Smoking or non-smoking?

Posto sul corridoio o vicino al finestrino?
Window seat or aisle seat?

Posso vedere il vostro passaporto/biglietto, per favore?
Can I see your passport/ticket, please?

I passeggeri in partenza per Roma sono pregati di recarsi all'imbarco
Passengers for Rome are requested to board

Recarsi all'uscita quattro, per favore
Please proceed to gate number four

Biglietti, prego
Tickets please

Il treno intercity numero 687 per Roma è in partenza dal binario tre
Intercity train number 687 for Rome is leaving from platform three

Il treno regionale numero 89 da Bologna è in arrivo al binario due
Local train number 89 from Bologna is approaching platform two

Il treno espresso numero 435 da Venezia viaggia con trenta minuti di ritardo
Express train number 435 from Venice is running thirty minutes late

Apra la valigia, per favore
Open your suitcase, please

RESTAURANTS

There are various types of places for eating out. For snacks the most common is the bar. These are open all day from early morning until about 10 pm. They are all licensed to sell alcohol and usually offer a variety of sandwiches, rolls, cakes and hot and cold drinks. In most bars you are required to go first to the cash desk, make your order, pay and get a receipt (**scontrino**) which you then hand to the barman and repeat your order. You will notice that most Italians stand up in bars – sitting down costs extra. The sign **tavola calda** means that hot dishes are also served.

For full meals there are **osteria**, **pizzeria**, **trattoria**, **taverna** and **ristorante**. Wherever possible, it's a good idea to choose the **menu turistico** (tourist menu) or the **menu fisso** (set menu). Although the variety is more restricted, the food is of the same standard and you get a good deal more for your money, without having to face any service charge shocks at the end of the meal. Always ask for the local culinary specialities and local wine as they are generally excellent, and wine is a great deal cheaper and of superior quality in its place of origin.

In Italy, you can order the following types of coffee: **espresso** – strong black coffee; **caffè macchiato** – espresso with a dash of milk; **cappuccino** – frothy, milky coffee sprinkled with cocoa; **caffelatte** – white coffee. These are the most common but you also get **caffè corretto** – **espresso** with a liqueur; **caffè decaffeinato** – decaffeinated coffee; **caffè lungo** – weak **espresso**; **caffè ristretto** – strong **espresso**. Remember that if you ask for: '**Un caffè, per favore**', you will be served an **espresso**.

USEFUL WORDS AND PHRASES

beer	la birra	_beer_-ra
bill	il conto	_konto_
bottle	la bottiglia	bot-_teel_-ya
bread	il pane	_panay_
butter	il burro	_boor_-ro

café	il caffè	*kaf-<u>feh</u>*
cake	la torta	*<u>to</u>rta*
carafe	la caraffa	*kar<u>a</u>f-fa*
children's portion	una porzione per bambini	*portz-<u>yo</u>nay pair bamb<u>ee</u>nee*
coffee	il caffè	*kaf-<u>feh</u>*
cup	la tazza	*t<u>a</u>tza*
dessert	il dessert	*'dessert'*
fork	la forchetta	*fork<u>e</u>t-ta*
glass	il bicchiere	*beek-<u>ya</u>iray*
half-litre	da mezzo litro	*da m<u>e</u>tzo l<u>ee</u>tro*
knife	il coltello	*kolt<u>e</u>l-lo*
litre	un litro	*l<u>ee</u>tro*
main course	il piatto principale	*p-y<u>a</u>t-to preencheep<u>a</u>lay*
menu	il menù	*mayn<u>oo</u>*
milk	il latte	*l<u>a</u>t-tay*
pepper	il pepe	*p<u>ay</u>pay*
plate	il piatto	*p-y<u>a</u>t-to*
receipt *(in bars)*	lo scontrino	*skontr<u>ee</u>no*
(in restaurants)	la ricevuta	*reechev<u>oo</u>ta*
restaurant	il ristorante	*reestor<u>a</u>ntay*
salt	il sale	*s<u>a</u>lay*
sandwich	il panino	*pan<u>ee</u>no*
serviette	il tovagliolo	*toval-y<u>o</u>lo*
snack	lo spuntino	*spoont<u>ee</u>no*
soup	la minestra	*meen<u>e</u>stra*
spoon	il cucchiaio	*kook-y<u>a</u>-yo*
starter	l'antipasto	*anteep<u>a</u>sto*
sugar	lo zucchero	*dz<u>oo</u>kairo*
table	il tavolo	*t<u>a</u>volo*
tea	il tè	*teh*
teaspoon	il cucchiaino	*kook-ya-<u>ee</u>no*
tip	la mancia	*m<u>a</u>ncha*
waiter	il cameriere	*kamair-y<u>ai</u>ray*
waitress	la cameriera	*kamair-y<u>ai</u>ra*
water	l'acqua	*<u>a</u>kwa*

wine	il vino	*veeno*
wine list	la lista dei vini	*leesta day veenee*

A table for one/two/three please
Un tavolo per una persona/per due/per tre, per favore
oon tavolo pair oona pairsona/pair doo-ay/pair tray pair favoray

Can I see the menu/wine list?
Potrei vedere il menu/la lista dei vini?
potray vedairay eel maynoo/la leesta day veenee

What would you recommend?
Cosa ci consiglia?
koza chee konseel-ya

I'd like ...
Vorrei...
vor-ray

Just an espresso/cappuccino/white coffee, please
Solo un caffè/un cappuccino/un caffelatte, per favore
solo oon kaf-feh/oon kap-poocheeno/oon kaf-faylat-tay pair favoray

I only want a snack
Vorrei solo uno spuntino
vor-ray solo oono spoonteeno

Is there a set menu?
C'è un menù fisso?
cheh oon maynoo fees-so

Can we try a local speciality/wine?
Potremmo assaggiare una specialità/un vino locale?
potrem-mo as-saj-jaray oona spech-yaleeta/oon veeno lokalay

A litre of house red, please
Un litro di vino rosso della casa, per favore
oona leetro dee veeno ros-so del-la kaza pair favoray

Do you have any vegetarian dishes?
Avete piatti vegetariani?
avetay p-yat-tee vejetar-yanee

Could we have some water?
Potremmo avere un po' d'acqua?
potrem-mo avairay oon po dakwa

Is there a children's menu?
C'è un menù per bambini?
cheh oon maynoo pair bambeenee

Waiter/waitress!
Cameriere/cameriera!
kamair-yairay/kamair-yaira

We didn't order this!
Non lo abbiamo ordinato!
non lo abb-yamo ordeenato

You've forgotten to bring my dessert
Ha dimenticato di portarmi il dessert
a deementeekato dee portarmee eel 'dessert'

May we have some more ...?
Potremmo avere ancora un po' di...?
potrem-mo avairay ankora oon po dee

Can I have another knife/spoon?
Potrei avere un altro coltello/cucchiaio?
potray avairay oon altro koltel-lo/kook-ya-yo

Can we have the bill, please?
Può portarci il conto, per favore?
pwo portarchee eel konto pair favoray

Could I have a receipt, please?
Potrei avere la ricevuta/lo scontrino, per favore?
potray avairay la reechevoota/lo skontreeno pair favoray

Can we pay separately?
Possiamo pagare separatamente?
poss-yamo pagaray separatamentay

That was very good, thank you
Era ottimo, grazie
aira ot-teemo gratzee-ay

YOU MAY HEAR

Buon appetito!
Enjoy your meal!

Cosa vuole da bere?
What would you like to drink?

Avete mangiato bene?
Did you enjoy your meal?

MENU GUIDE

abbacchio alla romana	Roman-style spring lamb
acciughe sott'olio	anchovies in oil
aceto	vinegar
acqua	water
acqua minerale gassata	sparkling mineral water
acqua minerale non gassata	still mineral water
acqua naturale	still mineral water, tap water
affettato misto	variety of cold, sliced meats such as salami, cooked ham etc
affogato al caffè	ice cream with hot *espresso* coffee poured over it
aglio	garlic
agnello	lamb
agnello al forno	roast lamb
albicocche	apricots
ananas	pineapple
anatra	duck
anatra all'arancia	duck in orange sauce
anguilla in umido	stewed eel
anguria	water melon
antipasti	starters
antipasti misti	variety of starters
aperitivo	aperitif
aragosta	lobster
arancia	orange
aranciata	orangeade
aringa	herring
arista di maiale al forno	roast chine of pork
arrosto di tacchino	roast turkey
arrosto di vitello	roast veal
asparagi	asparagus
avocado all'agro	avocado pears with oil and lemon or vinegar
baccalà	dried cod
baccalà alla vicentina	Vicentine-style dried cod
bagnacauda	vegetables (usually raw) in an oil, garlic and anchovy sauce
barbaresco	dry, red wine from the Piedmont region

63

barbera	dry red wine from Piedmont
bardolino	dry red wine from area around Verona
barolo	dark, dry red wine from Piedmont
basilico	basil
bavarese	ice-cream cake with cream
bel paese	soft, full-fat white cheese
besciamella	white sauce
bignè	cream puff
birra	beer
birra chiara	light beer, lager
birra grande	large beer *(approx. 1 pint)*
birra piccola	small beer *(approx. $^1/_2$ pint)*
birra scura	dark beer
bistecca (di manzo)	beef steak
bistecca ai ferri	grilled steak
bollito misto	assorted boiled meats with vegetables
braciola di maiale	pork steak
branzino al forno	baked sea bass
brasato	braised beef with herbs
bresaola	dried, salted beef sliced thinly and eaten cold with oil and lemon
brioche	type of croissant
brodo	clear broth
brodo di pollo	chicken broth
brodo vegetale	clear, vegetable broth
budino	pudding
burro	butter
burro di acciughe	anchovy butter
caciotta	tender, white, medium-fat cheese from Central Italy
caffè	coffee
caffè corretto	*espresso* coffee with a dash of liqueur
caffè lungo	weak *espresso* coffee
caffè macchiato	*espresso* coffee with a dash of milk
caffè ristretto	strong *espresso* coffee
caffellatte	half coffee, half hot milk
calamari in umido	stewed squid
calamaro	squid
calzone	folded pizza with tomato and mozzarella or *ricotta* inside

camomilla	camomile tea
cannella	cinnamon
cannelloni al forno	rolls of egg pasta stuffed with meat and baked in the oven
cappelle di funghi porcini alla griglia	grilled boletus mushroom caps
cappuccino	*espresso* coffee with foaming milk and a sprinkling of cocoa powder
capretto al forno	roast kid
carciofi	artichokes
carciofini sott'olio	baby artichokes in oil
carne	meat
carote	carrots
carpaccio	finely-sliced beef fillets with oil, lemon and grated parmesan
carré di maiale al forno	roast pork loin
cassata siciliana	Sicilian ice-cream cake with glacé fruit, chocolate and *ricotta*
castagne	chestnuts
cavoletti di Bruxelles	Brussels sprouts
cavolfiore	cauliflower
cavolo	cabbage
cefalo	mullet
cernia	grouper *(fish)*
charlotte	ice-cream cake with milk, eggs, cream, biscuits and fruit
chianti	dark red Tuscan wine
ciambella	ring-shaped cake
cicoria	chicory
cicorino	small chicory plants
ciliege	cherries
cime di rapa	young leaves of turnip plant
cioccolata	chocolate
cioccolata calda	hot chocolate
cipolle	onions
cocktail di gamberetti	prawn cocktail
conchiglie alla marchigiana	pasta shells in tomato sauce with celery, carrot, parsley and ham
coniglio	rabbit
coniglio arrosto	roast rabbit
coniglio in salmí	jugged rabbit

coniglio in umido	stewed rabbit
consommé	clear broth made with meat or chicken
contorni	vegetables
coperto	cover charge
coppa	cured neck of pork, sliced finely and eaten cold
costata alla fiorentina	Florentine entrecôte
costata di manzo	beef entrecôte
cotechino	spiced pork sausage for boiling
cotoletta	veal, pork or lamb chop
cotoletta ai ferri	grilled veal or pork chop
cotoletta alla milanese	veal chop in breadcrumbs
cotoletta alla valdostana	veal chop with ham and cheese cooked in breadcrumbs
cotolette di agnello	lamb chops
cotolette di maiale	pork chops
cozze	mussels
cozze alla marinara	mussels in seafood sauce
crema	custard dessert made with eggs and milk
crema al caffè	coffee custard dessert
crema al cioccolato	chocolate custard dessert
crema di funghi	cream of mushroom soup
crema di piselli	cream of pea soup
crema pasticciera	confectioner's custard
crêpe suzette	pancake flambéed with orange sauce
crescente	type of flat, fried Emilian bread made with flour, lard and eggs
crespelle	type of savoury pancake filled with white sauce and other fillings
crespelle ai funghi	savoury pancakes with mushrooms
crespelle al formaggio	savoury pancakes with cheese
crespelle al pomodoro	savoury pancakes with tomato
crostata di frutta	fruit tart
dadi	stock cubes
datteri	dates
degustazione	tasting
degustazione di vini	wine tasting
denominazione di origine controllata (DOC)	guarantee of quality of wine

dentice al forno	baked dentex *(type of sea bream)*
digestivo	digestive liqueur
dolci	sweets, desserts, cakes
endivia belga	Belgian endives
entrecôte (di manzo)	beef entrecôte
espresso	strong black coffee
fagiano	pheasant
fagioli	beans
fagioli borlotti in umido	fresh borlotti beans *(type of kidney bean)* cooked in vegetables, herbs and tomato sauce
fagiolini	long, green beans
faraona	guinea fowl
fegato	liver
fegato alla veneta	liver cooked in butter with onions
fegato con salvia e burro	liver cooked in butter and sage
fettuccine	ribbon-shaped pasta
fettuccine al salmone	*fettuccine* with salmon
fettuccine panna e funghi	*fettuccine* with cream and mushrooms
fichi	figs
filetti di pesce persico	fillets of perch
filetti di sogliola	fillets of sole
filetto (di manzo)	fillet of beef
filetto ai ferri	grilled fillet of beef
filetto al cognac	fillet of beef in cognac
filetto al pepe verde	fillet of beef with green pepper
filetto al sangue	rare fillet of beef
filetto ben cotto	well-done fillet of beef
filetto medio	medium fillet of beef
finocchio	fennel
finocchi gratinati	fennel with melted, grated cheese
fonduta	cheese fondue
formaggi misti	variety of cheeses
fragole	strawberries
fragole con gelato/panna	strawberries and ice cream/cream
frappé	whisked fruit or milk drink with crushed ice
frappé al cioccolato	chocolate milk shake
frascati	dry, white wine from area around Rome
frittata	type of omelette

frittata al formaggio	cheese omelette
frittata al prosciutto	ham omelette
frittata alle erbe	herb omelette
frittata alle verdure	vegetable omelette
fritto misto	mixed seafood in batter
frittura di pesce	variety of fried fish
frutta	fruit
frutta alla fiamma	fruit flambé
frutta secca	dried nuts and raisins
frutti di bosco	mixture of strawberries, raspberries, mulberries etc
frutti di mare	seafood
funghi	mushrooms
funghi trifolati	mushrooms fried in garlic and parsley
gamberetti	shrimps
gamberi	prawns
gamberoni	king prawns
gazzosa	clear lemonade
gelatina	gelatine
gelato	ice cream
gelato con panna	ice cream with cream
gelato di crema	vanilla-flavoured ice cream
gelato di frutta	fruit-flavoured ice cream
gnocchetti verdi agli spinaci e al gorgonzola	small flour, potato and spinach dumplings with melted gorgonzola
gnocchi	small flour and potato dumplings
gnocchi alla romana	small milk and semolina dumplings baked with butter
gnocchi al pomodoro	small flour and potato dumplings in tomato sauce
gorgonzola	strong, soft blue cheese from Lombardy
grancevola	spiny spider crab
granchio	crab
granita	drink with crushed ice
granita di caffè	iced coffee
granita di caffè con panna	iced coffee with cream
granita di limone	lemon drink with crushed ice
grigliata di pesce	grilled fish
grigliata mista	mixed grill *(meat or fish)*
grissini	thin, crisp breadsticks

gruviera	Gruyère cheese
indivia	endive
insalata	salad
insalata caprese	salad of sliced tomatoes and mozzarella
insalata di funghi porcini	boletus mushroom salad
insalata di mare	seafood salad
insalata di nervetti	boiled beef or veal served cold with beans and pickles
insalata di pomodori	tomato salad
insalata di riso	rice salad
insalata mista	mixed salad
insalata russa	Russian salad
insalata verde	green salad
involtini	meat rolls stuffed with ham and herbs
lamponi	raspberries
lamponi con gelato/panna	raspberries and ice cream/cream
lasagne al forno	layers of thick, flat pasta baked in tomato sauce, mince and cheese
latte	milk
latte macchiato con cioccolato	hot, foamy milk with a sprinkling of cocoa powder
lattuga	lettuce
leggero	light
legumi	pulses
lemonsoda	sparkling lemon drink
lenticchie	lentils
lepre	hare
limonata	lemon-flavoured fizzy drink
limone	lemon
lingua	tongue
lingua salmistrata	ox tongue marinaded in brine and then cooked
macedonia di frutta	fruit salad
macedonia di frutta al maraschino	fruit salad in Maraschino
macedonia di frutta con gelato	fruit salad with ice cream
maiale	pork
maionese	mayonnaise
mandarino	mandarin
mandorla	almond

manzo	beef
marroni	chestnuts
marsala	very sweet wine similar to sherry
marzapane	marzipan
medaglioni di vitello	veal medallions
mela	apple
melanzane	aubergines
melanzane alla siciliana	baked aubergine slices with parmesan, tomato sauce and egg
melone	melon
menta	mint
menu turistico	tourist menu
meringata	meringue pie
meringhe con panna	meringues with cream
merlot	dark red wine of French origin
merluzzo	cod
merluzzo alla pizzaiola	cod in tomato sauce with anchovies, capers and parsley
merluzzo in bianco	boiled cod with oil and lemon
messicani in gelatina	rolls of veal in gelatine
millefoglie	layered pastry slice with confectioners' custard
minestra in brodo	noodle soup
minestrone	thick vegetable soup with rice or *vermicelli*
mirtilli	bilberries
mirtilli con gelato/panna	bilberries and ice cream/cream
more	mulberries or blackberries
more con gelato/panna	mulberries or blackberries and ice cream/cream
moscato	sweet, sparkling wine
mostarda di Cremona	preserve of glacé fruit in grape must or sugar with syrup and mustard
mousse al cioccolato	chocolate mousse
mozzarella	firm, white, milky buffalo cheese
mozzarella in carrozza	slices of bread and mozzarella coated in flour and fried
nasello	hake
noce moscata	nutmeg
nocciole	hazelnuts
noci	walnuts

nodino	veal chop
olio	oil
orata al forno	baked gilthead *(fish)*
origano	oregano
ossobuco	stewed shin of veal
ostriche	oysters
paglia e fieno	mixture of plain and green *tagliatelle*
paillard di manzo	slices of grilled beef
paillard di vitello	slices of grilled veal
pane	bread
panino	filled roll
panna	cream
parmigiana di melanzane	baked dish of aubergines, tomato sauce, mozzarella and parmesan
parmigiano	parmesan cheese
pasta al forno	pasta baked in white sauce and grated cheese
pasta e fagioli	very thick soup with puréed borlotti beans and small pasta rings
pasta e piselli	pasta with peas
pasticcio di fegato d'oca	baked, pasta-covered dish with goose liver
pasticcio di lepre	baked, pasta-covered dish with hare
pasticcio di maccheroni	baked macaroni
pastina in brodo	noodle soup
patate	potatoes
patate al forno	baked potatoes
patate arrosto	roast potatoes
patate fritte	chips
patate in insalata	potato salad
pâté di carne	pâté
pâté di fegato	liver pâté
pâté di pesce	fish pâté
pecorino	strong, hard ewe's milk cheese
penne	pasta quills
penne ai quattro formaggi	pasta quills with sauce made from four cheeses
penne all'arrabbiata	pasta quills with tomato and chilli pepper sauce
penne panna e prosciutto	pasta quills with cream and ham sauce

pepe	pepper *(spice)*
peperoni	peppers
peperoni ripieni	stuffed peppers
peperoni sott'olio	peppers in oil
pera	pear
pesca	peach
pesca melba	peach melba
pesce	fish
pesce al cartoccio	fish baked in foil with herbs
pesce in carpione	marinaded fish
pinot	dry white wine from the Veneto region
pinzimonio	assorted whole, raw vegetables eaten with oil and vinegar
piselli	peas
piselli al prosciutto	fresh peas cooked in clear broth, butter, ham and basil
pizza Margherita	pizza with tomato and mozzarella
pizza napoletana	pizza with tomato, mozzarella and anchovies
pizza quattro stagioni	pizza with tomato, mozzarella, ham, mushrooms and artichokes
pizzaiola	slices of cooked beef in tomato sauce, oregano and anchovies
pizzoccheri alla Valtellinese	thin, pasta strips with green vegetables, melted butter and cheese
polenta	yellow cornmeal boiled in water with salt, then left to set and cut in slices
polenta e funghi	*polenta* with mushrooms
polenta e latte	*polenta* with milk
polenta e osei	*polenta* with small birds
polenta pasticciata	alternate layers of *polenta*, tomato sauce and cheese
pollo	chicken
pollo alla cacciatora	chicken in white wine and mushroom sauce
pollo alla diavola	chicken pieces flattened and deep-fried
pollo al forno/arrosto	roast chicken
polpette	meatballs
polpettone	meatloaf

pomodori	tomatoes
pomodori ripieni	stuffed tomatoes
pompelmo	grapefruit
porri	leeks
prezzemolo	parsley
primi piatti	first courses
prosciutto cotto	cooked ham
prosciutto crudo/di Parma	type of cured ham
prosciutto di Praga	cooked ham
prosciutto e fichi	cured ham with figs
prosciutto e melone	cured ham with melon
prugne	plums
punte di asparagi all'agro	asparagus tips in oil and lemon
purè di patate	creamed potatoes
quaglie	quails
radicchio	chicory
ragù	sauce made with mince, tomatoes and diced vegetables
rapa	type of white turnip with flavour similar to radish
rapanelli	radishes
ravioli	small, square-shaped egg pasta filled with meat or cheese
ravioli al pomodoro	ravioli stuffed with meat, in tomato sauce
razza	skate
ricotta	type of cottage cheese
risi e bisi	*risotto* with peas and small pieces of ham
riso	rice
riso al pomodoro	rice with tomato
riso in brodo	rice in clear broth
riso in insalata	rice salad
risotto	rice cooked in stock
risotto ai funghi	mushroom *risotto*
risotto al nero di seppia	black *risotto* made with cuttlefish ink
risotto al salmone	salmon *risotto*
risotto al tartufo	truffle *risotto*
risotto alla castellana	*risotto* with mushroom, ham, cream and cheese sauce
risotto alla milanese	*risotto* flavoured with saffron

roast-beef all'inglese	roast beef (sliced very thinly and served cold with lemon)
robiola	type of soft cheese from Lombardy
rognone trifolato	small kidney pieces in garlic, oil and parsley
rosatello/rosato	rosé wine
rosmarino	rosemary
salame	salami
sale	salt
salmone affumicato	smoked salmon
salsa cocktail	mayonnaise and ketchup sauce for garnishing fish and seafood
salsa di pomodoro	tomato sauce
salsa tartara	tartar sauce
salsa vellutata	white sauce made with clear broth instead of milk
salsa verde	sauce for meats made with chopped parsley and oil
salsiccia	sausage
salsiccia di cinghiale	wild boar sausage
salsiccia di maiale	pork sausage
saltimbocca alla romana	slices of veal rolled with ham and sage and fried
salvia	sage
sambuca (con la mosca)	aniseed-flavour liqueur from Lazio region served with a coffee bean in the glass
sarde ai ferri	grilled sardines
scaloppine	veal escalopes
scaloppine ai carciofi	veal escalopes with artichokes
scaloppine ai funghi	veal escalopes with mushrooms
scaloppine al Marsala	veal escalopes in Marsala
scaloppine al prezzemolo	veal escalopes with parsley
scaloppine al vino bianco	veal escalopes in white wine
scamorza alla griglia	grilled soft cheese
scampi alla griglia	grilled scampi
secco	dry
secondi piatti	second courses, main courses
sedano di Verona	Veronese celery
selvaggina	game
semifreddo	dessert made of ice cream and sponge

senape	mustard
seppie in umido	stewed cuttlefish
servizio compreso	service charge included
servizio escluso	not including service charge
soave	dry white wine from region around Lake Garda
sogliola	sole
sogliola ai ferri	grilled sole
sogliola al burro	sole cooked in butter
sogliola alla mugnaia	sole cooked in flour and butter
sorbetto	sorbet, soft ice cream
soufflé al formaggio	cheese soufflé
soufflé al prosciutto	ham soufflé
spaghetti	spaghetti
spaghetti aglio, olio e peperoncino	spaghetti with garlic, oil and crushed chilli pepper
spaghetti al pesto	spaghetti in crushed basil, garlic, oil and parmesan dressing
spaghetti al pomodoro	spaghetti in tomato sauce
spaghetti al ragù	spaghetti with mince and tomato sauce
spaghetti alla carbonara	spaghetti with egg, chopped bacon and cheese sauce
spaghetti alla puttanesca	spaghetti with anchovies, capers and black olives in tomato sauce
spaghetti alle vongole	spaghetti with clams
spaghetti all'matriciana	spaghetti in minced pork and tomato sauce typical of Rome
speck	type of cured, smoked ham
spezzatino di vitello	veal stew
spiedini	small pieces of assorted meats or fish cooked on a spit
spinaci	spinach
spinaci all'agro	spinach with oil and lemon
spremuta d'arancia	freshly squeezed orange juice
spremuta di limone	freshly squeezed lemon juice
spumante	sparkling wine
stracchino	type of soft cheese from Lombardy
stracciatella	beaten eggs cooked in boiling, clear broth
strudel di mele	apple strudel

succo d'arancia	orange juice
succo di albicocca	apricot juice
succo di pera	pear juice
succo di pesca	peach juice
succo di pompelmo	grapefruit juice
sugo al tonno	tomato sauce with garlic, tuna and parsley
svizzera	hamburger
tacchino ripieno	stuffed turkey
tagliata	finely-cut beef fillet cooked in the oven
tagliatelle	thin, flat strips of egg pasta
tagliatelle al basilico	*tagliatelle* and chopped basil
tagliatelle alla bolognese	*tagliatelle* with mince and tomato sauce
tagliatelle al pomodoro	*tagliatelle* with tomato sauce
tagliatelle al ragù	*tagliatelle* with mince and tomato sauce
tagliatelle con panna e funghi	*tagliatelle* with cream and mushroom sauce
tagliatelle rosse	*tagliatelle* with chopped red peppers
tagliatelle verdi	*tagliatelle* with chopped spinach
tagliolini	thin, soup noodles
tagliolini ai funghi	*tagliolini* with mushrooms
tagliolini alla panna	*tagliolini* with cream
tagliolini al salmone	*tagliolini* with salmon
tartine	small sandwiches
tartufo	round ice cream covered in cocoa or chocolate
tè	tea
tè con latte	tea with milk
tè con limone	lemon tea
tiramisù	dessert made with coffee-soaked sponge, eggs, Marsala cream and cocoa powder
tonno	tuna
torta	tart, flan
torta salata	savoury flan
torta ai carciofi	artichoke flan
torta al cioccolato	chocolate tart
torta al formaggio	cheese flan

torta di mele	apple tart
torta di noci	walnut tart
torta di ricotta	type of cheesecake
torta di zucchine	courgette flan
torta gelato	ice-cream tart
tortellini	small pasta shapes filled with minced pork, ham, parmesan and nutmeg
tortellini alla panna	*tortellini* with cream
tortellini al pomodoro	*tortellini* with tomato sauce
tortellini al ragù	*tortellini* with mince and tomato sauce
tortellini in brodo	*tortellini* in clear broth
tortelloni di magro/di ricotta	pasta shapes filled with cheese, parsley, chopped vegetables
tortelloni di zucca	*tortelloni* stuffed with pumpkin
trancio di palombo	smooth hound slice *(fish)*
trancio di pesce spada	swordfish steak
trenette col pesto	type of flat spaghetti with crushed basil, garlic, oil and cheese sauce
triglie	mullet *(fish)*
trippa	tripe
trota	trout
trota affumicata	smoked trout
trota al burro	trout cooked in butter
trota alle mandorle	trout with almonds
trota bollita	boiled trout
uccelletti	small birds wrapped in bacon, served on cocktail sticks
uova	eggs
uova al tegamino con pancetta	fried eggs and bacon
uova alla coque	boiled eggs
uova farcite	eggs with tuna, capers and mayonnaise filling
uova sode	hard-boiled eggs
uva	grapes
uva bianca	white grapes
uva nera	black grapes
vellutata di asparagi	creamed asparagus with egg yolks
vellutata di piselli	creamed peas with egg yolks
verdura	vegetables
vermicelli	very fine, thin pasta, often used in soups

vino	wine
vino bianco	white wine
vino da dessert	dessert wine
vino da pasto	table wine
vino da tavola	table wine
vino rosso	red wine
vitello	veal
vitello tonnato	sliced veal in blended tuna, anchovy, oil and lemon sauce
vongole	clams
würstel	frankfurter
zabaione	creamy dessert made from beaten eggs, sugar and Marsala
zafferano	saffron
zucca	pumpkin
zucchine	courgettes
zucchine al pomodoro	chopped courgettes in tomato, garlic and parsley sauce
zucchine ripiene	stuffed courgettes
zuccotto	ice-cream cake with sponge, cream and chocolate
zuppa	soup
zuppa di cipolle	onion soup
zuppa di cozze	mussel soup
zuppa di lenticchie	lentil soup
zuppa di pesce	fish soup
zuppa di verdura	vegetable soup
zuppa inglese	trifle

SHOPS AND SERVICES

This chapter covers all sorts of shopping needs and services, and to start with you'll find some general phrases which can be used in lots of different places – many of which are named in the list below. After the general phrases come some more specific requests and sentences to use when you've found what you need, be it food, clothing, repairs, film-developing, a haircut or haggling in the market. Don't forget to refer to the mini-dictionary for items you may be looking for.

Shops are usually open from 8.30/9 am to 12.30/1 pm and from 3.30/4 pm to 7.30/8 pm and often later in tourist resorts in the high season. Shop hours may vary slightly according to the region you are in and shops may close on different days of the week – often on Monday mornings, all day Monday or on Thursday afternoons. Venice has half-day closing (only in winter) on Monday mornings. In Florence, shops are closed on Monday mornings or all day Monday in winter, autumn and spring and are closed on Saturday afternoons in August. Most large shops and supermarkets are open Monday to Saturday.

It's acceptable to haggle in the market but only if the price is not displayed.

In Italy, **chili** (kilos) and **etti** (hectograms) are used. One **etto** = 100 grams. Cheese, ham etc are generally sold by the **etto** and fruit and vegetables by the kilo.

There are some differences between Italian and British shops. Chemists are very expensive (see HEALTH page 113). So if you should need items such as antiseptic, toothpaste, plasters, tampons etc then it's better to·go to a supermarket or to a **drogheria** (*drogairee-a*), which is like a chemist's and general grocery store combined. If you wish to buy perfumes or sophisticated cosmetic products, you should go to a **profumeria** (*profoomairee-a*). If you want to buy films or get your photos developed go to a photographic shop or an optician's, NOT to a chemist's.

In Italy you won't find the type of launderette where you can do your own washing and drying. A dry cleaner's will only accept clothes for dry-cleaning or large items such as bed linen, but not small personal items.

For cigarettes, stamps, chewing gum and postcards go to a **tabaccaio** which can be identified by a white **T** on a black background. A **tabaccaio** generally has the same opening hours as shops. After 7.30/8 pm, you can only buy cigarettes in specially licensed bars or in railway stations.

USEFUL WORDS AND PHRASES

antique shop	il negozio di antiquariato	*negotz-yo dee anteekwar-yato*
audio equipment shop	il negozio di hi-fi	*negotz-yo dee 'hi-fi'*
baker's	la panetteria	*panet-tairee-a*
boutique	la boutique	*booteek*
bookshop	la libreria	*leebrairee-a*
butcher's	la macelleria	*machel-lairee-a*
buy	comprare	*kompraray*
cake shop	la pasticceria	*pasteechairee-a*
camera shop	il negozio di macchine fotografiche	*negotz-yo dee mak-keenay fotografeekay*
camping equipment	l'attrezzatura da campeggio	*at-tretz-zatoora da kampej-jo*
carrier bag	il sacchetto	*sak-ket-to*
cheap	economico	*ekonomeeko*
chemist's	la farmacia	*farmachee-a*
china	la porcellana	*porchel-lana*
confectioner's	la pasticceria	*pasteech-chairee-a*
cost	costare	*kostaray*
craft shop	il negozio di artigianato	*negotz-yo dee arteejanato*
department store	il grande magazzino	*granday magatzeeno*
dry cleaner's	la lavanderia a secco, la tintoria	*lavandairee-a a sek-ko, teentoree-a*

80

electrical goods store	il negozio di articoli elettrici	*negotz-yo dee arteekolee elet-treechee*
expensive	caro, costoso	*karo, kostozo*
fishmonger's	la pescheria	*peskairee-a*
florist's	il negozio di fiori	*negotz-yo dee f-yoree*
food store	il negozio di generi alimentari	*negotz-yo dee jaynairee aleementaree*
fruit	la frutta	*froot-ta*
gift shop	il negozio di articoli da regalo	*negotz-yo dee arteekolee da raygalo*
greengrocer's	il negozio di frutta e verdura	*negotz-yo dee froot-ta ay verdoora*
grocer's	il negozio di alimentari	*negotz-yo dee aleementaree*
hairdresser's		
(men's)	barbiere	*l urb-yairay*
(women's)	parrucchiere, acconciature	*ʀ-rookk-yairay, ʀ-konchatooray*
hardware shop	la ferramenta	*jair-ramenta*
hypermarket	l'ipermercato	*eepairmairkato*
indoor market	il mercato coperto	*mairkato kopairto*
jeweller's	la gioielleria	*joyel-lairee-a*
ladies' wear	l'abbigliamento per signora	*ab-beel-yamento pair seen-yora*
market	il mercato	*mairkato*
menswear	l'abbigliamento da uomo	*ab-beel-yamento da wommo*
newsagent's	la rivendita di giornali	*reevendeeta dee jornalee*
optician's	il negozio di ottica	*negotz-yo dee ot-teeka*
pharmacy	la farmacia	*farmachee-a*
receipt	lo scontrino	*skontreeno*
record shop	il negozio di dischi	*negotz-yo dee deeskee*
sale	la svendita, i saldi	*zvendeeta, saldee*
shoe repairer's	la calzoleria	*kaltzolairee-a*
shoe shop	il negozio di scarpe	*negotz-yo dee skarpay*
shop	il negozio	*negotz-yo*

souvenir shop	il negozio di souvenir	*negotz-yo dee sooveneer*
sports equipment	l'attrezzatura sportiva	*at-tretz-zatoora sporteeva*
sportswear	l'abbigliamento sportivo	*ab-beel-yamento sporteevo*
stationer's	la cartoleria	*kartolairee-a*
supermarket	il supermercato	*soopairmairkato*
tailor	il sarto	*sarto*
till	la cassa	*kas-sa*
tobacconist's	la tabaccheria	*tabak-kairee-a*
toyshop	il negozio di giocattoli	*negotz-yo dee jokat-tolee*
travel agent's	l'agenzia di viaggio	*ajentzee-a dee vee-aj-jo*
vegetables	la verdura	*vairdoora*
wine merchant's	la bottiglieria	*bot-teel-yairee-a*

Excuse me, where is/where are ...?
Mi scusi, dov'è/dove sono...?
mee skoozee doveh/dovay sono

Where is there a ... (shop)?
Dov'è un negozio di... qui vicino?
doveh oon negotz-yo dee ... kwee veecheeno

Where is the ... department?
Dov'è il reparto...?
doveh eel reparto

Where is the main shopping area?
Dov'è la zona dei negozi?
doveh la zona day negotzi

Is there a market here?
C'è un mercato qui?
cheh oon mairkato kwee

I'd like ...
Vorrei...
vor-ray

Do you have ...?
Avete...?
avaytay

How much is this?
Quanto costa questo?
kwanto kosta kwesto

Where do I pay?
Dove si paga?
dovay see paga

Do you take credit cards?
Accettate carte di credito?
ach-chet-tatay kartay dee kraydeeto

I think perhaps you've short-changed me
Penso che abbiate sbagliato di darmi il resto
penso kay abb-yatay sbal-yato dee darmee eel resto

Can I have a receipt/a bag, please?
Potrebbe darmi lo scontrino/un sacchetto?
potrayb-bay darmee lo skontreeno/oon sak-ket-to

I'm just looking
Sto solo dando un'occhiata
sto solo dando oon okk-yata

I'll come back later
Tornerò più tardi
tornairo p-yoo tardee

Do you have any more of these?
Ne ha ancora di questi?
nay a ankora dee kwestee

Have you anything cheaper?
Non ha niente di più economico?
non a n-yentay dee p-yoo ekonomeeko

Have you anything larger/smaller?
Non ne ha uno più grande/piccolo?
non nay a oono p-yoo granday/peek-kolo

Can I try it/them on?
Posso provarlo/provarli?
pos-so provarlo/provarlee

Does it come in other colours?
C'è anche in altri colori?
cheh ankay een altree koloree

Could you gift-wrap it for me?
Può farmi un pacchetto regalo?
pwo farmee oon pak-ket-to raygalo

I'd like to exchange this, it's faulty
Vorrei cambiare questo: è difettoso
vor-ray kamb-yaray kwesto: eh deefet-tozo

I'm afraid I don't have the receipt
Mi dispiace, ma non ho lo scontrino
mee deesp-yachay ma non oh lo skontreeno

Can I have a refund?
Posso riavere indietro i soldi?
pos-so ree-avairay endee-aytro ee soldee

My camera isn't working
La mia macchina fotografica non funziona
la mee-a mak-keena fotografeeka non foontz-yona

I want a 36-exposure colour film. 100ISO
Vorrei una pellicola 100ISO a colori da 36 foto
vor-ray oona pel-leekola 100 ee-ess-oh a koloree da 36 foto

I'd like this film processed
Vorrei sviluppare questa pellicola
vor-ray sveeloop-paray kwesta pel-leekola

Matt/glossy prints
Fotografie su carta opaca/lucida
fotografee-ay soo karta opaka/loocheeda

One-hour service, please
Vorrei il servizio in un'ora, per favore
vor-ray eel serveetz-yo een oon ora pair favoray

Where can I get this mended?
Dove posso farlo riparare?
dovay pos-so farlo reepararay

Can you mend this?
Può aggiustarmelo?
pwo aj-joostarmaylo

I'd like this skirt/these trousers dry-cleaned
Vorrei far pulire questa gonna/questi pantaloni
vor-ray far pooleeray kwesta gon-na/kwestee pantalonee

When will it/they be ready?
Quando sarà pronto/saranno pronti?
kwando sara pronto/saran-no prontee

I'd like to make an appointment
Vorrei prendere un appuntamento
vor-ray prendairay oon ap-poontamento

I want a cut and blow-dry
Vorrei taglio e messa in piega (con il föhn)
vor-ray tal-yo ay mes-sa een p-yayga kon eel fon

With conditioner/No conditioner, thanks
Con il balsamo/Senza il balsamo, grazie
kon eel bal-samo/sentza eel bal-samo gratzee-ay

Just a trim, please
Solo una spuntatina, per favore
solo oona spoontateena pair favoray

Not too much off!
Non tagli troppo!
non tal-yee trop-po

When does the market open?
Quando apre il mercato?
kwando apray eel mairkato

What's the price per kilo?
Quanto costa al chilo?
kwanto kosta al keelo

Could you write that down?
Può scriverlo?
pwo skreevairlo

That's too much! I'll pay ...
È troppo! Lo do...
eh trop-po! lo do

Could I have a discount?
Potrebbe farmi uno sconto?
potrayb-bay farmee oono skonto

That's fine. I'll take it
Va bene. Lo prendo!
va baynay. lo prendo

I'll have a piece of that cheese
Vorrei un pezzo di quel formaggio
vor-ray oon petz-zo dee kwel formaj-jo

About 250/500 grams
Circa duecentocinquanta/cinquecento grammi
cheerka doo-ay-chentocheenkwanta/cheenkwaychento gram-mee

A kilo/half a kilo of apples, please
Un chilo/mezzo chilo di mele, per favore
oon keelo/metzo keelo dee maylay pair favoray

250 grams of that cheese, please
Due etti e mezzo di quel formaggio, per favore
doo-ay et-tee ay metzo dee kwel formaj-jo pair favoray

May I taste it?
Posso assaggiarlo?
pos-so as-saj-jarlo

That's very nice, I'll take some
Quello è molto buono; ne prenderò un po'
kwel-lo eh molto bwono; nay prayndairo oon po

It isn't what I wanted
Non è quello che volevo
non eh kwel-lo kay volayvo

THINGS YOU'LL SEE

abbigliamento da uomo	men's clothing
abbigliamento per signora	ladies' clothing
acconciature	ladies' hairdresser
agenzia di viaggio	travel agency
alimentari	groceries
barbiere	barber's
calzature	shoes
cartoleria	stationer's
cassa	cash desk, till
coiffeur	hair stylist
colpi di sole	highlights
dolci	confectionery, cakes
dozzina	dozen
elettrodomestici	electrical appliances
entrata	way in

→

fai-da-te	DIY
fioraio	flower shop
forniture per ufficio	office supplies
fresco	fresh
giocattoli	toys
grande magazzino	department store
la merce venduta non si cambia senza lo scontrino	goods are not exchanged without a receipt
libreria	bookshop
liquori	spirits
macelleria	butcher's
messa in piega con il föhn	blow-dry
moda	fashion
munitevi di un carrello/cestino	please take a trolley/basket
pagare alla cassa	pay at the desk
panetteria	bakery
parrucchiere (per signora)	ladies' hairdresser
pasticceria	cake shop
pellicceria	furrier
permanente	perm
pescheria	fish market
piano superiore	upper floor
prezzo	price
prima qualità	high quality
reparto	department
ribassato/ridotto	reduced
riviste	magazines
saldi	sales
salone da parrucchiere	hairdressing salon
salone per uomo	men's hairdresser
sartoria	tailor's
spingere	push
spuntata	trim
svendita	sale
tabacchi	tobacco

→

taglio	cut
tirare	pull
uscita	exit
verdure	vegetables

THINGS YOU'LL HEAR

Desidera?
Can I help you?

La stanno servendo?
Are you being served?

Non ha spiccioli?
Haven't you anything smaller? *(money)*

Mi dispiace quest'articolo è esaurito
I'm sorry, we're out of stock

Questo è tutto quello che abbiamo
This is all we have

Ha spiccioli/moneta?
Do you have any change?

Diamo solamente buoni acquisto
We only give credit notes

Si accomodi alla cassa, prego
Please pay at the till

Niente altro?
Will there be anything else?

Quanto ne vuole?
How much would you like?

Come lo desidera?
How would you like it?

SPORT

Whether you enjoy sport as a passive spectator or as an active participant, Italy has a great deal to offer. The Italians are passionate football fans and the championships are played from September to May, with some international matches in June and July. Cycling is also a favourite Italian sport and the **Giro d'Italia** – the annual race round the peninsula – takes place during May and June.

Summer sports include fishing, golf, skin diving, swimming and tennis. There is no lack of fine beaches in Italy and most of them are well-managed and provide everything for the tourist's enjoyment. There are numerous windsurfing schools where you can take lessons and hire all the necessary equipment, from boards to wetsuits. One of the most notable areas for this sport is Lake Garda.

Italy is a haven for mountain climbers and hill-walkers who will delight in discovering the many beautiful Alpine and Apennine valleys unknown to the average tourist. For winter sports there are excellently equipped skiing resorts in the Dolomites and in the Piedmont and Lombardy regions of Northern Italy.

USEFUL WORDS AND PHRASES

athletics	l'atletica	*atlayteeka*
ball	la palla	*pal-la*
bicycle	la bicicletta	*beecheeklet-ta*
binding *(ski)*	l'attacco (degli sci)	*at-tak-ko del-yee shee*
cable car	la funivia	*fooneevee-a*
canoe/canoeing	la canoa	*kano-a*
chair lift	la seggiovia	*sej-jovee-a*
cross-country skiing	lo sci di fondo	*shee dee fondo*
cycling	il ciclismo	*cheekleezmo*
go cycling	andare in bicicletta	*andaray een beecheeklet-ta*
dive	tuffarsi	*toof-farsee*

diving board	il trampolino	_trampoleeno_
downhill skiing	lo sci da discesa	_shee da deeshayza_
fishing	la pesca	_peska_
fishing rod	la canna da pesca	_kan-na da peska_
flippers	le pinne	_peen-nay_
football _(sport)_	il calcio	_kalcho_
(ball)	il pallone	_pal-lonay_
football match	la partita di calcio	_parteeta dee kalcho_
game _(match)_	la partita	_parteeta_
goggles	la maschera	_maskaira_
golf course	il campo da golf	_kampo da 'golf'_
play golf	giocare a golf	_jokaray a 'golf'_
gymnastics	la ginnastica	_jeen-nasteeka_
hang-gliding	il deltaplano	_deltaplano_
harpoon	l'arpione	_arp-yonay_
hunting	la caccia	_kach-cha_
ice-hockey	l'hockey su ghiaccio	_'hockey' soo g-yach-cho_
mast	l'albero	_albairo_
mountaineering	l'alpinismo	_alpeeneezmo_
nursery slope	la pista per	_peesta pair_
	principianti	_preencheep-yantee_
parascending	il parapendio	_parapendee-o_
oxygen bottles	le bombole di	_bombolay dee_
	ossigeno	_os-seejeno_
pedal boat	il pedalò	_pedalo_
piste	la pista	_peesta_
racket	la racchetta	_rak-ket-ta_
ride	andare a cavallo	_andaray a kaval-lo_
riding	l'equitazione	_aykweetatz-yonay_
riding hat	il cappello da fantino	_kap-pel-lo da fanteeno_
rock climbing	la roccia	_roch-cha_
saddle	la sella	_sel-la_
sail	la vela	_vayla_
sailboard	il surf	_'surf'_
sailing	la vela	_vayla_
go sailing	fare vela	_faray vayla_
shooting range	il tiro a segno	_teero a sen-yo_

skate	pattinare	*pat-teenaray*
skates	i pattini	*pat-teenee*
skating rink	la pista di pattinaggio	*peesta dee pateenaj-jo*
ski	sciare	*shee-aray*
ski boots	gli scarponi da sci	*skarponee da shee*
skiing	lo sci	*shee*
skin diving	l'immersione subacquea	*eem-mairsjonay soobakway-a*
ski pass	lo ski pass	*'ski pass'*
skis	gli sci	*shee*
skisticks	i bastoncini	*bastoncheenee*
ski tow	lo skilift	*'skilift'*
ski trail	la pista da sci	*peesta da shee*
ski wax	la sciolina	*shee-oleena*
sledge	la slitta	*zleeta*
snorkel	il respiratore a tubo	*respeeratoray a toobo*
sports centre	il centro sportivo	*chentro sporteevo*
stadium	lo stadio	*stad-yo*
surfboard	il surf	*surf*
swim	nuotare	*nwotaray*
swimming pool	la piscina	*peesheena*
team	la squadra	*skwadra*
tennis court	il campo da tennis	*kampo da ten-nis*
toboggan	la slitta	*zleeta*
underwater fishing	la pesca subacquea	*peska soobakway-a*
volleyball	la pallavolo	*pal-lavolo*
water-ski	fare sci d'acqua	*faray shee dakwa*
water-skiing	lo sci d'acqua	*shee dakwa*
water-skis	gli sci d'acqua	*shee dakwa*
wet suit	la muta da sub	*moota da soob*
go windsurfing	praticare il windsurf	*prateekaray eel 'windsurf'*

How do I get to the beach?
Potrebbe indicarmi la strada per la spiaggia?
potrayb-bay eendeekarmee la strada pair la sp-yaj-ja

How deep is the water here?
Quant'è profonda qui l'acqua?
kwanteh profonda kwee lakwa

Is there an indoor/outdoor pool here?
C'è una piscina coperta/scoperta?
cheh oona peesheena kopairta/skopairta

Is it dangerous to swim here?
È pericoloso nuotare qui?
eh paireekolozo nwotaray kwee

Can I fish here?
Posso pescare qui?
pos-so peskaray kwee

Do I need a licence?
C'è bisogno della licenza?
cheh beezon-yo del-la leechentza

Is there a golf course near here?
C'è un campo da golf da queste parti?
cheh oon kampo da 'golf' da kwestay partee

Do I have to be a member?
È necessario essere socio?
eh neches-sar-yo es-sairay socho

Where can I hire …?
Dove posso noleggiare...?
dovay pos-so nolej-jaray

I would like to hire a bike/some skis
Vorrei noleggiare una bicicletta/degli sci
vor-ray nolej-jaray oona beecheeklet-ta/del-yee shee

How much does it cost per hour/day?
Quanto costa all'ora/al giorno?
kwanto kosta al ora/al jorno

When does the lift start?
A che ora aprono gli impianti?
a kay ora aprono l-yee eemp-yantee

What are the snow conditions like today?
Quali sono le condizioni della neve oggi?
kwalee sono lay kondeetz-yonee del-la nayvay oj-jee

How much is a daily/weekly lift pass?
Quanto costa un abbonamento giornaliero/settimanale?
kwanto kosta oon ab-bonamento jornal-yairo/set-tee-manalay

I would like to take skiing lessons
Vorrei prendere lezioni di sci
vor-ray prendairay letz-yonee dee shee

Where are the nursery slopes?
Dove sono le discese per principianti?
dovay sono lay deeshayzay pair preencheep-yantee

Is it very steep?
È molto ripido?
eh molto reepeedo

I would like to take water-skiing lessons
Vorrei prendere lezioni di sci d'acqua
vor-ray prendairay letz-yonee dee shee dakwa

There's something wrong with this binding
C'è qualcosa che non va in questo attacco
cheh kwalkoza kay non va een kwesto at-tak-ko

I haven't played this before
Non ho mai provato prima
non oh mɪ provato preema

Let's go skating/swimming
Andiamo a pattinare/sciare
and-yamo a pat-teenaray/shee-aray

What's the score?
A quanto sono?
a kwanto sono

Who won?
Chi ha vinto?
kee a veento

THINGS YOU'LL SEE

alla seggiovia	to the chair lift
correnti pericolose	dangerous currents
divieto di balneazione	no bathing
divieto di pesca	no fishing
funivia	cable car
noleggio barche	boat hire
noleggio biciclette	cycle hire
noleggio sci	ski hire
non dondolarsi	no swinging
pedoni	pedestrians
pericolo	danger
pericolo di valanghe	danger of avalanches
piscina coperta	indoor swimming pool
piscina scoperta	open-air swimming pool
pista ciclabile	cycle path
pista da fondo	cross-country ski track
pista facile/difficile	easy/difficult slope
pista per slitte	toboggan run
prepararsi a scendere	get ready to alight
pronto soccorso	first aid
sci di fondo	cross-country skiing
scuola di sci	ski school
trampolino	diving board; ski jump
vietato bagnarsi	no bathing
vietato pescare	no fishing
vietato tuffarsi	no diving

95

POST OFFICES AND BANKS

Main post offices are open from 8.15 am to 7 pm, while local offices generally close at 2 pm. Post boxes in Italy are generally red, although there are some yellow ones. Stamps can be bought at the post office or, more conveniently, at any **tabaccaio** (tobacconist's). These are easily identifiable by the sign displayed outside – a white **T** on a black background.

Banks are open from 8.30 am to 1.30 pm and from 2.45 pm to 3.45 pm, from Monday to Friday. Generally speaking, it is better to change money in a bank than in a bureau de change (called **cambio** or **cambiavalute**), because the latter charge a commission. Bureaux de change are to be found in airports, in railway stations and in the city centre. In larger cities, you will find automatic bureaux de change with cash dispensers outside some banks.

You will find cash dispensers for Eurocheques and for credit cards outside the main banks (but a commission of about 5% is charged if you draw money with a credit card). Major credit cards are generally accepted in hotels, restaurants and shops, but not always. Small shops or restaurants do not accept them.

The Italian currency is the **lira** (plural **lire**, abbreviation **L.**). There are coins of 10, 20, 50, 100, 200 and 500 lire, and banknotes of 1,000, 2,000, 5,000, 10,000, 50,000 and 100,000 lire.

USEFUL WORDS AND PHRASES

airmail	la posta aerea	p_o_sta a-_a_iray-a
bank	la banca	b_a_nka
banknote	la banconota	bankon_o_ta
cash	il denaro	den_a_ro
cash dispenser	lo sportello automatico	sport_e_l-lo owtom_a_teeko
change	cambiare	kamb-y_a_ray
cheque	l'assegno	as-s_e_n-yo

cheque book	il libretto degli assegni	*leebret-to del-yee as-sen-yee*
collection	la levata	*levata*
counter	lo sportello	*sportel-lo*
credit card	la carta di credito	*karta dee kraydeeto*
customs form	il modulo per la dogana	*modoolo pair la dogana*
delivery	la consegna	*konsen-ya*
deposit *(noun)*	il deposito	*daypozeeto*
(verb)	depositare	*daypozeetaray*
envelope	la busta	*boosta*
exchange rate	il tasso di cambio	*tas-so dee kam-bee-o*
fax *(noun)*	il fax	*'fax'*
(verb: document)	spedire via fax	*spedeeray vee-a 'fax'*
fax machine	il fax	*'fax'*
form	il modulo	*modoolo*
international money order	il vaglia postale internazionale	*val-ja postalay eentairnatz-yonalay*
letter	la lettera	*let-taira*
mail	la posta	*posta*
money order	il vaglia postale	*val-ja postalay*
package/parcel	il pacchetto, il pacco	*pak-ket-to, pak-ko*
post *(noun)*	la posta	*posta*
(verb)	spedire	*spedeeray*
postage rates	le tariffe postali	*tareef-fay postalee*
postal order	il vaglia postale	*val-ya postalay*
post box	la cassetta delle lettere	*cas-set-ta del-lay let-tairay*
postcard	la cartolina	*kartoleena*
postcode	il codice di avviamento postale	*kodeechay dee avv-yamento postalay*
poste-restante	fermo posta	*fairmo posta*
postman	il postino	*posteeno*
post office	l'ufficio postale	*oof-feecho postalay*
pound sterling	la lira sterlina	*leera stairleena*
registered letter	la raccomandata	*rak-komandata*
stamp	il francobollo	*frankobol-lo*

97

surface mail	la posta ordinaria	*posta ordeenaree-a*
telegram	il telegramma	*telegram-ma*
traveller's cheque	il traveller's cheque	*'traveller's cheque'*
withdraw	prelevare	*praylevaray*
withdrawal	il prelievo	*praylyayvo*

How much is a postcard to England?
Quanto costa spedire una cartolina in Inghilterra?
kwanto kosta spedeeray oona kartoleena een eengeeltair-ra

I would like three 750-lira stamps
Vorrei tre francobolli da settecentocinquanta lire
vor-ray tray frankobol-lee da set-tay-chentocheenkwanta leeray

I want to register this letter
Vorrei spedire questa lettera per raccomandata
vor-ray spedeeray kwesta let-taira pair rak-komandata

I want to send this parcel to Scotland
Vorrei spedire questo pacco in Scozia
vor-ray spedeeray kwesto pak-ko een skotz-ya

How long does the post to America take?
Quanto ci mette la posta per arrivare in America?
kwanto chee met-tay la posta pair ar-reevaray een amaireeka

Where can I post this?
Dove posso imbucarlo?
dovay pos-so eembookarlo

Is there any mail for me?
C'è posta per me?
cheh posta pair may

I'd like to send a telegram/a fax
Vorrei spedire un telegramma/un fax
vor-ray spedeeray oon telegram-ma/oon 'fax'

98

This is to go airmail
Deve essere spedito per via aerea
dayvay es-sairay spaydeeto pair vee-a a-airay-a

I'd like to change this into 10,000 lire notes
Vorrei cambiare in banconote da diecimila
vor-ray kamb-yaray een bankonotay da dee-aycheemeela

Can I cash these traveller's cheques?
Posso cambiare questi traveller's cheques?
pos-so kamb-yaray kwestee 'traveller's cheques'

What is the exchange rate for the pound?
Qual è il tasso di cambio della sterlina?
kwaleh eel tas-so dee kam-bee-o del-la stairleena

Can I draw cash using this credit card?
Posso fare un prelievo usando la carta di credito?
pos-so faray oon prayl-yayvo oozando la karta dee kraydeeto

I'd like it in 50,000 lire notes
Vorrei banconote da cinquantamila
vor-ray bankonotay da cheenkwantameela

Could you give me smaller notes?
Può darmi banconote di piccolo taglio?
pwo darmee bankonotay dee peek-kolo tal-yo

THINGS YOU'LL SEE

affrancatura	postage
affrancatura per l'estero	postage abroad
assicurata	insured mail
cambiavalute/cambio	bureau de change
cartolina	postcard

→

codice (di avviamento) postale	postcode
compilare	to fill in
conto corrente	current account
deposito	deposit
destinatario	addressee
espresso	express
fermo posta	poste restante
francobollo	stamp
indirizzo	address
lettera	letter
orario di apertura	opening hours
mittente	sender
pacchetto	package
posta	mail
posta aerea	airmail
prelievo	withdrawal
raccomandata	registered letter
riempire	to fill in
sportello	counter
sportello pacchi	parcels counter
tariffa	rate, charge
tariffa interna	inland postage
telegrammi	telegrams

TELEPHONES

Old telephone boxes can be operated with 100 and 200 lire pieces or **gettoni** – tokens each worth 200 lire. But they are being replaced with phones that take 100, 200, 500 lire and tokens or phonecards (costing 5,000 or 10,000 lire) which can be bought at tobacconists. You can also use **gettoni** as normal currency, so don't be alarmed if you receive one in your change when shopping. When you need **gettoni** you can ask for them in any bar. If you need to make a long-distance phone call it is better to go to an office of the Italian national telephone company, the **SIP**, or to the **ASST** (**Azienda Statale Servizi Telefonici**) which is a department of the main post office in Florence and Venice. Alternatively, you can ask in a bar if the barman has **un telefono a scatti** – you make your call first and are then charged for the number of units you have used.

To telephone the UK, dial 00 44 followed by the area code (but exclude the 0 which prefixes all UK area codes) and the number you want. To call a USA number, dial 001 followed by the area code and the subscriber's number.

The tones you'll hear when telephoning in Italy are:

Dialling tone: two tones, one short and one long, at regular intervals;
Ringing tone: one single, long tone at regular intervals;
Engaged and unobtainable: short rapid pips.

USEFUL WORDS AND PHRASES

call *(noun)*	la telefonata	*telefon<u>a</u>ta*
(verb)	telefonare	*telefon<u>a</u>ray*
cardphone	il telefono a scheda	*telefono a sk<u>ay</u>da*
code	il prefisso	*pref<u>ee</u>s-so*
crossed line	l'interferenza	*eentairfair<u>e</u>ntza*
dial	fare il numero	*f<u>a</u>ray eel n<u>oo</u>mairo*
dialling tone	il segnale di libero	*sen-y<u>a</u>lay dee l<u>ee</u>bairo*
emergency	l'emergenza	*emairj<u>e</u>ntza*

enquiries	il servizio informazioni telefoniche	*sairveetz-yo eenformatz-yonee telefoneekay*
extension	l'interno	*eentairno*
international call	la chiamata internazionale	*k-yamata eentairnatz-yonalay*
number	il numero	*noomairo*
operator	l'operatore	*opairatoray*
payphone	il telefono a gettoni	*telefono a jet-tonee*
phonecard	la scheda telefonica	*skayda telefoneeka*
receiver	il ricevitore	*reecheveetoray*
reverse charge call	la chiamata a carico del destinatario	*k-yamata a kareeko del desteenataree-o*
telephone	il telefono	*telefono*
telephone box	la cabina telefonica	*kabeena telefoneeka*
telephone directory	la guida telefonica	*gweeda telefoneeka*
wrong number	il numero sbagliato	*noomairo zbal-yato*

Where is the nearest phone box?
Dov'è la cabina telefonica più vicina?
doveh la kabeena telefoneeka p-yoo veecheena

Is there a telephone directory?
C'è una guida telefonica?
cheh oona gweeda telefoneeka

I would like the directory for Venice
Vorrei la guida telefonica di Venezia
vor-ray la gweeda telefoneeka dee venetz-ya

Can I call abroad from here?
Posso fare una telefonata internazionale da qua?
pos-so faray oona telefonata eentairnatz-yonalay da kwa

I would like to reverse the charges
La metta a carico del destinatario
la met-ta a kareeko del desteenataree-o

I would like a number in Rome
Ho bisogno del numero di un abbonato di Roma
oh beezon-yo del noomairo dee oon ab-bonato dee roma

Can you give me an outside line?
Può darmi una linea esterna?
pwo darmee oona leenay-a estairna

How do I get an outside line?
Come devo fare per avere una linea esterna?
komay dayvo faray pair avairay oona leenay-a estairna

Hello, this is Anna speaking
Pronto, sono Anna
pronto sono an-na

Is that Mario?
Parlo con Mario?
parlo kon mar-yo

Speaking
Sono io/ All'apparecchio
sono ee-o/al-lap-parek-kyo

I would like to speak to Paola
Vorrei parlare con Paola
vor-ray parlaray kon paola

Extension 34 please, please
Interno trentaquattro, per favore
eentairno trentakwat-tro pair favoray

Please tell him/her Marina called
Per cortesia, gli/le dica che ha telefonato Marina
pair kortezee-a l-yee/lay deeka kay a telefonato mareena

Ask him/her to call me back please
Gli/le dica di ritelefonarmi, per favore
l-yee/lay deeka dee reetelefonarmee pair favoray

My number is 753522
Il mio numero è sette cinque tre cinque due due
eel mee-o noomairo eh set-tay cheenkway tray cheenkway doo-ay doo-ay

Do you know where he/she is?
Non sa dov'è?
non sa doveh

When will he/she be back?
Quando tornerà?
kwando tornaira

Could you leave him/her a message?
Potrebbe lasciargli/lasciarle un messaggio?
potrayb-bay lasharl-yee/lasharlay oon mes-saj-jo

I'll ring back later
Ritelefonerò più tardi
reetelefonairo p-yoo tardee

Sorry, I've got the wrong number
Mi scusi, ho sbagliato numero
mee skoozee oh zbal-yato noomairo

You've got the wrong number
Ha sbagliato numero
a zbal-yato noomairo

THE ALPHABET

a	*ah*	h	*ak-ka*	o	*o*	v	*voo*
b	*bee*	i	*ee*	p	*pee*	w	*voo dopp-yo*
c	*chee*	j	*ee-loonga*	q	*koo*	x	*eeks*
d	*dee*	k	*kap-pa*	r	*air-ay*	y	*eepseelon*
e	*ay*	l	*el-lay*	s	*es-say*	z	*tsay-ta*
f	*ef-fay*	m	*em-may*	t	*tee*		
g	*jee*	n	*en-nay*	u	*oo*		

REPLIES YOU MAY BE GIVEN

Pronto
Hello

Sono io/All'apparecchio
Speaking

Con chi vuole parlare?
Who would you like to speak to?

Ha sbagliato numero
You've got the wrong number

Chi parla?
Who's calling?

Attenda in linea, prego
Hold the line, please

Mi dispiace, non c'è
I'm sorry, he/she's not in

Posso richiamarla?
Can I call you back?

Che numero ha?
What is your number?

Tornerà alle...
He/she'll be back at ... o'clock

Richiami domani, per favore
Please call again tomorrow

Gli dirò che ha chiamato
I'll tell him you called

THINGS YOU'LL SEE

apparecchio	phone
cabina telefonica	telephone box
centralino	local exchange, operator
chiamata	call
chiamata in teleselezione	direct dialling
chiamata interurbana	long-distance call
chiamata urbana	local call
comporre il numero	dial
fuori servizio	out of order
gettoni	telephone tokens
guida telefonica	telephone directory
il servizio è gratuito	free service
inserire le monete	insert coins
moneta	coin
numeri utili	useful numbers
numero	number
Pagine Gialle	Yellow Pages
prefissi telefonici	codes
riagganciare	hang up
ricevitore	receiver
scatto	unit
scheda telefonica	phonecard
selezionare il numero	dial the number
servizio guasti	faults service
sollevare	to lift
vigili del fuoco	fire brigade

EMERGENCIES

Information on local health services can be obtained from tourist information offices but in an emergency, dial 113, which is a general emergency number (like 999 in Britain). Dial 115 for the fire brigade and 118 for an ambulance.

Remember that there is more than one type of police force in Italy: **carabinieri** are a military force and **polizia** are a civil force dealing with crime. In case of emergency, dial either 113 for **polizia** or 112 for **carabinieri**.

For emergency breakdown services dial 116 (or 01 in the provinces of Potenza, Catanzaro, Lecce or Caltanisetta) and you will be put in contact with the **ACI** (Italian Automobile Club) who will provide immediate assistance. There is an agreement between **ACI** and foreign automobile associations, so that members of the British AA or RAC can turn to **ACI** in an emergency (see also MOTORING page 37).

USEFUL WORDS AND PHRASES

accident	l'incidente	*eencheedentay*
ambulance	l'ambulanza	*amboolantza*
assault	aggredire	*ag-gredeeray*
breakdown	il guasto	*gwasto*
break down	guastarsi	*gwastarsee*
burglar	il ladro	*ladro*
burglary	il furto	*foorto*
casualty department	il pronto soccorso	*pronto sok-korso*
crash *(noun)*	l'incidente	*eencheedentay*
(verb)	avere un incidente	*avairay oon eencheedentay*
emergency	l'emergenza	*emairjentza*
fire *(flames)*	il fuoco	*fwoko*
(event)	l'incendio	*eenchend-yo*
fire brigade	i vigili del fuoco	*veejeelee del fwoko*

107

flood	l'inondazione	*eenondatz-yonay*
injured	ferito	*faireeto*
lose	perdere	*pairdairay*
pickpocket	il borsaiolo	*borsi-olo*
police	la polizia	*poleetzee-a*
police station	il commissariato di polizia	*kom-mees-sar-yato dee poleetzee-a*
rob	derubare	*dairoobaray*
steal	rubare	*roobaray*
theft	il furto	*foorto*
thief	il ladro	*ladro*
tow	rimorchiare	*reemork-yaray*

Help!
Aiuto!
I-ooto

Look out!
(Stia) attento!
(stee-a) at-tento

Stop!
Si fermi!
see fairmee

This is an emergency!
Questa è un'emergenza!
kwesta eh oon emairjentza

Get an ambulance!
Chiami un'ambulanza!
k-yamee oon amboolantza

Hurry up!
Presto!
presto

Please send an ambulance to …
Per favore, mandate un'ambulanza a…
pair favoray mandatay oon amboolantza a

Please come to …
Venite, per favore, a…
veneetay pair favoray a

My address is …
Il mio indirizzo è…
eel mee-o eendeereetzo eh

We've had a break-in
Ci sono entrati i ladri in casa
chee sono entratee ee ladree een kaza

There's a fire at …
C'è un incendio a…
cheh oon eenchend-yo a

Someone's been injured
C'è un ferito
cheh oon faireeto

Someone's been knocked down
È stata investita una persona
eh stata eenvesteeta oona pairsona

He's passed out
È svenuto
eh svenooto

My passport/car has been stolen
Mi hanno rubato il passaporto/la macchina
mee an-no roobato eel pas-saporto/la mak-keena

I've lost my traveller's cheques
Ho perso i miei traveller's cheques
oh pairso ee mee-ay 'traveller's cheques'

I want to report a stolen credit card
Vorrei denunciare il furto di una carta di credito
vor-ray denooncharay eel foorto dee oona karta dee kraydeeto

It was stolen from my room
È stato rubato dalla mia camera
eh stato roobato dal-la mee-a kamaira

I lost it in the park/at the station
L'ho perso nel parco/alla stazione
lo pairso nel parko/al-la statz-yonay

My luggage has gone missing
I miei bagagli sono spariti
ee mee-ay bagal-yee sono spareetee

Has my luggage been found yet?
Sono stati ritrovati i miei bagagli?
sono statee reetrovatee ee mee-ay bagal-yee

I've crashed my car/had a crash
Ho avuto un incidente con la macchina
oh avooto oon eencheedentay kon la mak-keena

My car's been broken into
La mia macchina è stata forzata
la mee-a mak-keena eh stata fortzata

The registration number is ...
Il numero di targa è...
eel noomairo dee targa eh

I've been mugged *(said by a man)*
Sono stato aggredito
sono stato ag-gredeeto

(said by a woman)
Sono stata aggredita
sono stata ag-gredeeta

My son's missing
Mio figlio è scomparso
mee-o feel-yo eh skomparso

He has fair/brown hair
Ha i capelli biondi/castani
a ee kapel-lee b-yondee/kastanee

He's ... years old
Ha... anni
a ... an-nee

I've locked myself out *(said by a man)*
Sono rimasto chiuso fuori
sono reemasto k-yoozo fworee

(said by a woman)
Sono rimasta chiusa fuori
sono reemasta k-yooza fworee

He's drowning!
Sta annegando!
sta an-negando

He/she can't swim!
Non sa nuotare!
non sa nwotaray

THINGS YOU'LL SEE

carabinieri	police
commissariato di polizia	police station
emergenza sanitaria	ambulance
farmacia di turno	late-night chemist's
numeri di emergenza	emergency phone numbers
ospedale	hospital
polizia	police

→

polizia stradale	traffic police
pronto intervento	emergency service
pronto soccorso	first aid
soccorso alpino	mountain rescue
soccorso stradale	breakdown service
telefono	telephone
vigili del fuoco	fire brigade

THINGS YOU'LL HEAR

Il suo/vostro indirizzo, prego?
What's your address, please?

Dove si trova/vi trovate?
Where are you?

Può descriverlo?
Can you describe it/him?

HEALTH

Under EC Social Security regulations visitors from the UK qualify for free medical treatment on the same basis as the Italians themselves. If you want to make sure of being in possession of all necessary documentation, you should obtain a T4 from a main post office, fill in the attached E111 and get it stamped at the post office before travelling. With the E111, you'll also get a leaflet explaining how to obtain treatment. Once in Italy you can get information from the Local Health Unit, the **USL** (**Unità Sanitaria Locale**).

If you should need medical treatment, hand your E111 to the **USL** and you will be given a certificate of entitlement. Ask to see a list of the scheme's doctors. You will be entitled to treatment from any of these, free of charge. For prescribed medicines a standard charge will be made at the chemist's (see also SHOPS AND SERVICES page 79). If you do not get the certificate from the Local Health Unit, you will have to pay for treatment and getting refunds later can be much more problematic. In any case the refund would only be partial. If a doctor thinks you need hospital treatment, he will give you a certificate (**proposta di ricovero**). This entitles you to free treatment in certain hospitals, a list of which will be available at the **USL**. If you cannot contact the **USL** office before going into hospital, show the E111 to the hospital authorities and ask them to get in touch with the **USL** about your right to free treatment.

If you need dental treatment in Italy, you should be prepared to pay. Most dentists are private and it could take months to get free treatment from the **USL**.

USEFUL WORDS AND PHRASES

accident	l'incidente	_eencheedentay_
ambulance	l'ambulanza	_amboolantza_
anaemic	anemico	_anaymeeko_
appendicitis	l'appendicite	_ap-pendeecheetay_
appendix	l'appendice	_ap-pendeechay_

aspirin	l'aspirina	*aspeereena*
asthma	l'asma	*azma*
backache	il mal di schiena	*mal dee sk-yayna*
bandage	la fascia, benda	*fasha, benda*
bite *(by dog, snake)*	il morso	*morso*
(by insect)	la puntura	*poontoora*
bladder	la vescica	*vesheeka*
blister	la vescica	*vesheeka*
blood	il sangue	*sangway*
blood donor	il donatore di sangue	*donatoray dee sangway*
burn	la bruciatura	*broo-chatoora*
cancer	il cancro	*kankro*
chemist	il farmacista	*farmacheesta*
chest	il petto	*pet-to*
chickenpox	la varicella	*vareechel-la*
cold	il raffreddore	*raf-fred-doray*
concussion	la commozione cerebrale	*kom-motz-yonay chairebralay*
constipation	la stitichezza	*steeteeketza*
contact lenses	le lenti a contatto	*lentee a kontat-to*
corn	il callo	*kal-lo*
cough	la tosse	*tos-say*
cut	il taglio	*tal-yo*
dentist	il dentista	*denteesta*
diabetes	il diabete	*dee-abaytay*
diarrhoea	la diarrea	*dee-aray-a*
doctor	il dottore, il medico	*dot-toray, medeeko*
earache	il mal d'orecchi	*mal dorek-kee*
fever	la febbre	*feb-bray*
filling	l'otturazione	*ot-tooratz-yonay*
first aid	il pronto soccorso	*pronto sok-korso*
flu	l'influenza	*eenfloo-entza*
fracture	la frattura	*frat-toora*
German measles	la rosolia	*rozolee-a*
haemorrhage	l'emorragia	*emor-rajee-a*
hayfever	il raffreddore da fieno	*raf-fred-doray da f-yeno*

headache	il mal di testa	*mal dee testa*
heart	il cuore	*kworay*
heart attack	l'infarto	*eenfarto*
hospital	l'ospedale	*ospedalay*
ill	malato	*malato*
indigestion	l'indigestione	*eendeejest-yonay*
injection	l'iniezione	*een-yetz-yonay*
itch	il prurito	*prooreeto*
kidney	il rene	*raynay*
lump	il nodulo	*nodoolo*
measles	il morbillo	*morbeel-lo*
migraine	l'emicrania	*emeekranee-a*
mumps	gli orecchioni	*orekk-yonee*
nausea	la nausea	*now-zay-a*
nurse	l'infermiera	*eenfairmee-aira*
(male)	l'infermiere	*eenfairmee-airay*
operation	l'operazione	*opairatz-yonay*
optician	l'ottico	*ot-teeko*
pain	il dolore	*doloray*
penicillin	la penicillina	*peneecheel-leena*
plaster	il cerotto	*chairot-to*
plaster of Paris	il gesso	*jes-so*
pneumonia	la polmonite	*polmoneetay*
pregnant	incinta	*eencheenta*
prescription	la ricetta	*reechet-ta*
rheumatism	il reumatismo	*ray-oomateezmo*
scald	la scottatura	*skot-tatoora*
scratch	il graffio	*graf-fee-o*
smallpox	il vaiolo	*vi-olo*
sore throat	il mal di gola	*mal dee gola*
splinter	la scheggia	*skej-ja*
sprain	la slogatura,	*zlogatura,*
	lo strappo muscolare	*strap-po mooskolaray*
sting	la puntura	*poontura*
stomach	lo stomaco	*stomako*
temperature	la febbre	*feb-bray*
tonsils	le tonsille	*tonseel-lay*

toothache	il mal di denti	*mal dee dentee*
travel sickness	il mal d'auto	*mal dowto*
ulcer	l'ulcera	*oolchaira*
vaccination	la vaccinazione	*vacheenatz-yonay*
vomit	vomitare	*vomeetaray*
whooping cough	la pertosse	*pairtos-say*

I have a pain in …
Mi fa male...
mee fa malay

I do not feel well
Non mi sento bene
non mee sento baynay

I feel faint
Mi sento svenire
mee sento zveneeray

I feel sick
Ho la nausea
oh la now-zay-a

I feel dizzy
Mi gira la testa
mee jeera la testa

It hurts here
Mi fa male qui
mee fa malay kwee

It's a sharp/dull pain
È un dolore acuto/sordo
eh oon doloray akooto/sordo

It hurts all the time
Mi fa continuamente male
mee fa konteenoo-amentay malay

It only hurts now and then
Non mi fa sempre male
non mee fa sempray malay

It hurts when you touch it
Mi fa male quando lo tocca
mee fa malay kwando lo tok-ka

It hurts more at night
Mi fa male di più di notte
mee fa malay dee p-yoo dee not-tay

It stings
Brucia
broocha

It aches
Fa male
fa malay

I have a temperature
Ho la febbre
oh la feb-bray

I need a prescription for ...
Avrei bisogno di una ricetta per...
avray beezon-yo dee oona reechet-ta pair

I normally take ...
Generalmente prendo...
jenairalmentay prendo

I'm allergic to ... *(said by a man/woman)*
Sono allergico/allergica a...
sono al-lairjeeko/al-lairjeeka a

Have you got anything for ...?
Ha qualcosa per...?
a kwalkoza pair

, a prescription for …?
…no della ricetta per…?
…on-yo del-la reechet-ta pair

I have lost a filling
Ho perso un'otturazione
oh pairso oon ot-tooratz-yonay

Will he/she be all right?
Starà bene?
stara baynay

Will he/she need an operation?
Dovrà essere operato/operata?
dovra essairay operato/operata

How is he/she?
Come sta?
komay sta

THINGS YOU'LL SEE

ambulanza	ambulance
anticamera	waiting room
autoambulanza	ambulance
chirurgia	surgery
chirurgo	surgeon
degente	in-patient
dermatologo	dermatologist
dottore	doctor
farmacia di turno	duty chemist's, late-night chemist's
ginecologo	gynaecologist
infermeria	infirmary
medico di turno	doctor on duty
oculista	oculist
orario di visita	visiting hours

→

ospedale	hospital
otorinolaringoiatra	ear, nose and throat specialist
ottico	optician
pronto soccorso	first aid, casualty ward
reparto	ward
sala operatoria	operating theatre
specialista	specialist

THINGS YOU'LL HEAR

Da inghiottire con acqua
With water

Da masticare
Chew them

Una/due/tre volte al giorno
Once/twice/three times a day

Prima di andare a letto
At bedtime

Al mattino
In the morning

Cosa prende normalmente?
What do you normally take?

Penso che lei debba andare dal medico
I think you should see a doctor

Mi dispiace, non ne abbiamo/vendiamo
I'm sorry, we don't have/sell that

Per questo c'è bisogno della ricetta
You need a prescription for that

CONVERSION TABLES

DISTANCES

A mile is 1.6km. To convert kilometres to miles, divide the km by 8 and multiply by 5. Convert miles to km by dividing the miles by 5 and multiplying by 8.

miles	0.62	1.24	1.86	2.43	3.11	3.73	4.35	6.21
miles or km	**1**	**2**	**3**	**4**	**5**	**6**	**7**	**10**
km	1.61	3.22	4.83	6.44	8.05	9.66	11.27	16.10

WEIGHTS

The kilogram is equivalent to 2lb 3oz. To convert kg to lbs, divide by 5 and multiply by 11. One ounce is about 28 grams, and eight ounces about 227 grams; 1lb is therefore about 454 grams.

lbs	2.20	4.41	6.61	8.82	11.02	13.23	19.84	22.04
lbs or kg	**1**	**2**	**3**	**4**	**5**	**6**	**9**	**10**
kg	0.45	0.91	1.36	1.81	2.27	2.72	4.08	4.53

TEMPERATURE

To convert Celsius degrees into Fahrenheit, the accurate method is to multiply the °C figure by 1.8 and add 32. Similarly, to convert °F to °C, subtract 32 from the °F figure and divide by 1.8.

°C	-10	0	5	10	20	30	36.9	40	100
°F	14	32	41	50	68	77	98.4	104	212

LIQUIDS

A litre is about 1.75 pints; a gallon is roughly 4.5 litres.

gals	0.22	0.44	1.10	2.20	4.40	6.60	11.00
gals or litres	**1**	**2**	**5**	**10**	**20**	**30**	**50**
litres	4.54	9.10	22.73	45.46	90.92	136.40	227.30

TYRE PRESSURES

lb/sq in	18	20	22	24	26	28	30	33
kg/sq cm	1.3	1.4	1.5	1.7	1.8	2.0	2.1	2.3

MINI-DICTIONARY

a un/uno/una/un' *(see page 5)*
about: about 16 circa 16
  a book about Venice un libro su
  Venezia
accelerator l'acceleratore
accident l'incidente
accommodation l'alloggio, il posto
ache il dolore
adaptor il riduttore
address l'indirizzo
adhesive l'adesivo
after dopo
afternoon il pomeriggio
aftershave il dopobarba
again di nuovo
against contro
Aids l'Aids
air l'aria
air-conditioning l'aria
  condizionata
aircraft l'aereo
airline la linea aerea
airport l'aeroporto
airport bus l'autobus navetta
alarm clock la sveglia
alcohol l'alcol
all tutto
  all the streets tutte le strade
  that's all questo è tutto
almost quasi
alone solo
Alps le Alpi
already già
always sempre
am: I am (io) sono
ambulance l'ambulanza
America l'America
American *(man)* l'americano
  (woman) l'americana

(adj) americano
and e
ankle la caviglia
anorak la giacca a vento
another un altro, un'altra
anti-freeze l'antigelo
antique shop il negozio di
  antiquariato
antiseptic l'antisettico
apartment l'appartamento
aperitif l'aperitivo
appetite l'appetito
apple la mela
application form il modulo per la
  domanda
appointment l'appuntamento
apricot l'albicocca
are: you are (Lei) è
  (singular, familiar) (tu) sei
  (plural) (voi) siete
  we are (noi) siamo
  they are (loro) sono
arm il braccio
arrive arrivare
art l'arte
art gallery la galleria d'arte
artist l'artista
as: as soon as possible (il) più
  presto possibile
ashtray il portacenere
asleep: he's asleep dorme
aspirin l'aspirina
at: at the post office all'ufficio
  postale
  at night di notte
  at 3 o'clock alle tre
attractive attraente
aunt la zia
Australia l'Australia

Australian *(man)* l'australiano
  (woman) l'australiana
  (adj) australiano
automatic automatico
away: is it far away? è lontano?
  go away! vattene!
awful terribile, orribile
axe l'ascia
axle il semiasse

baby il bambino
  (female) la bambina
back *(not front)* la parte posteriore
  (body) la schiena
  to come back tornare
bacon la pancetta
  bacon and eggs uova e pancetta
bad cattivo
bag la borsa
baggage claim il ritiro bagagli
bait l'esca
bake cuocere (al forno)
baker's la panetteria
balcony il balcone
ball *(football etc)* la palla
  (tennis etc) la pallina
banana la banana
band *(musicians)* la banda
bandage la fascia
bank la banca
banknote la banconota
bar *(drinks)* il bar
  bar of chocolate la tavoletta di
  cioccolata
barbecue il barbecue
  (occasion) la grigliata all'aperto
barber's il barbiere
bargain l'affare
basement il seminterrato
basin *(sink)* il lavabo
basket il cestino
  (in supermarket) il cestello
bath il bagno
  (tub) la vasca da bagno

to have a bath fare il bagno
bathroom il bagno
battery la batteria
beach la spiaggia
beans i fagioli
beard la barba
beautiful bello
because perché
bed il letto
bed linen le lenzuola
bedroom la camera da letto
beef il manzo
beer la birra
before ... prima di...
beginner il/la principiante
behind dietro
  behind ... dietro a...
beige beige
bell *(church)* la campana
  (door) il campanello
below sotto
belt la cintura
  (technical) la cinghia
beside ... vicino a...
best il migliore
better (than) migliore (di)
between ... fra...
bicycle la bicicletta
big grande
bikini il bikini
bill il conto
bin liner il sacchetto per la
  pattumiera
bird l'uccello
Biro ® la penna a sfera
birthday il compleanno
  happy birthday! buon
  compleanno!
biscuit il biscotto
bite *(noun: by dog)* il morso
  (by insect) la puntura
  (verb: by dog) mordere
  (by insect) pungere
bitter amaro

black nero
blackberry la mora
blackcurrant il ribes nero
blanket la coperta
bleach la varechina
  (verb: hair) ossigenare
blind *(cannot see)* cieco
  (on window) la tenda avvolgibile
blizzard la bufera di neve
blond(e) *(adj)* biondo
blood il sangue
blouse la camicetta
blue azzurro
  (darker) blu
boat la nave
  (small) la barca
  (passenger) il battello
body il corpo
boil *(verb: of water)* bollire
  (egg etc) far bollire
bolt *(noun: on door)* il catenaccio
  (verb) chiudere con il catenaccio
bone l'osso
  (fish) la lisca
bonnet *(car)* il cofano
book *(noun)* il libro
  (verb) prenotare
booking office la biglietteria
bookshop la libreria
boot *(car)* il portabagagli
  (footwear) lo stivale
border il confine
boring noioso
born: I was born in London sono nato a Londra
  I was born in 1965 sono nato nel 1965
both: both of them tutti e due
  both ... and ... sia... che...
bottle la bottiglia
bottle-opener l'apribottiglie
bottom il fondo
  (part of body) il sedere
  at the bottom (of) in fondo (a)

bowl la scodella
  (mixing bowl) la terrina
box la scatola
  (of wood etc) la cassetta
box office il botteghino
boy il ragazzo
boyfriend il ragazzo
bra il reggiseno
bracelet il braccialetto
braces le bretelle
brake *(noun)* il freno
  (verb) frenare
brandy il brandy
bread il pane
breakdown *(car)* il guasto
  (nervous) l'esaurimento nervoso
  I've had a breakdown *(car)* ho avuto un guasto
breakfast la colazione
breathe respirare
bridge il ponte
  the Bridge of Sighs il Ponte dei Sospiri
briefcase la cartella
British britannico
brochure l'opuscolo
broken rotto
  broken leg la gamba rotta
brooch la spilla
brother il fratello
brown marrone
bruise il livido
brush *(noun: hair)* la spazzola
  (paint) il pennello
  (cleaning) la scopa
  (verb: hair) spazzolare
bucket il secchio
building l'edificio
bumper il paraurti
burglar il ladro
burn *(noun)* la bruciatura
  (verb) bruciare
bus l'autobus, la corriera
business l'affare

it's none of your business non sono affari tuoi

bus station la stazione degli autobus

busy *(occupied)* occupato
(bar) animato

but ma

butcher's la macelleria

butter il burro

button il bottone

buy comprare

by: by the window vicino alla finestra
by Friday entro venerdì
by myself da solo
written by ... scritto da...

cabbage il cavolo

cable car la funivia

café il caffè, il bar

cagoule il K-way ®

cake la torta

cake shop la pasticceria

calculator il calcolatore

call: what's it called? come si chiama?

camcorder la videocamera

camera la macchina fotografica

campsite il campeggio

camshaft l'albero a camme

can *(tin)* la lattina

can: can I have ...? posso avere...?
can you ...? potreste...?
he/she can't ... non può...

Canada il Canada

Canadian *(man)* il canadese
(woman) la canadese
(adj) canadese

canal il canale

candle la candela

canoe la canoa

cap *(bottle)* il tappo
(hat) il berretto

car l'auto, la macchina

caravan la roulotte

carburettor il carburatore

card *(for birthday etc)* il biglietto
playing cards le carte da gioco

cardigan il cardigan

careful attento
be careful! stia attento!

caretaker il portinaio
(female) la portinaia

carpet il tappeto

carrot la carota

carry-cot il porte-enfant

case *(suitcase)* la valigia

cash *(noun)* il denaro
(verb) riscuotere
to pay cash pagare in contanti

cash dispenser lo sportello automatico

cassette la cassetta

cassette player il mangianastri

castle il castello

cat il gatto

cathedral la cattedrale

Catholic cattolico

cauliflower il cavolfiore

cave la grotta

cemetery il cimitero

central heating il riscaldamento centrale

centre il centro

certificate il certificato

chair la sedia

change *(noun: money)* il cambio
(verb: money, trains) cambiare
(clothes) cambiarsi

cheap economico, a buon mercato

check-in il check-in

check in fare il check-in

cheers! *(toast)* alla salute!, cin cin!

cheese il formaggio

chemist's la farmacia

cheque l'assegno

cheque book il libretto degli assegni

cheque card la carta assegni

cherry la ciliegia
chess gli scacchi
chest *(part of body)* il petto
(furniture) il baule
chest of drawers il cassettone
chewing gum il chewing-gum
chicken il pollo
child il bambino
(female) la bambina
children i bambini
china la porcellana
chips la patatine fritte
chocolate la cioccolata
box of chocolates una scatola di cioccolatini
chop *(food)* la costoletta
(verb: cut) tagliare (a pezzetti)
Christian name il nome di battesimo
church la chiesa
cigar il sigaro
cigarette la sigaretta
cinema il cinema
city la città
city centre il centro (della città)
class la classe
classical music la musica classica
clean *(adj)* pulito
clear *(obvious)* chiaro
(water) limpido
clever bravo, intelligente
cling film la pellicola adesiva
clock l'orologio
close *(near)* vicino (a)
(stuffy) soffocante
(verb) chiudere
closed chiuso
clothes i vestiti
clubs *(cards)* fiori
clutch la frizione
coach la corriera
(of train) la carrozza
coach station la stazione delle corriere

coat il capotto
coathanger l'attaccapanni
cockroach lo scarafaggio
coffee il caffè
coin la moneta
cold *(illness)* il raffreddore
(adj) freddo
I have a cold ho un raffreddore
Coliseum il Colosseo
collar il colletto
collection *(stamps etc)* la collezione
(postal) la levata
colour il colore
colour film la pellicola a colori
comb *(noun)* il pettine
(verb) pettinare
come venire
I come from ... sono di...
we came last week siamo arrivati la settimana scorsa
come here! vieni qui!
Common Market il Mercato Comune
compact disc il compact disc
compartment lo scompartimento
complicated complicato
computer il computer
concert il concerto
conditioner *(hair)* il balsamo
condom il preservativo
conductor *(bus)* il bigliettaio
(orchestra) il direttore
congratulations! congratulazioni!
consulate il consolato
contact lenses le lenti a contatto
contraceptive il contraccettivo
cook *(noun)* il cuoco
(female) la cuoca
(verb) cucinare
cooker il fornello
cooking utensils gli utensili da cucina
cool fresco
cork il tappo

corkscrew il cavatappi
corner l'angolo
corridor il corridoio
cosmetics i cosmetici
cost *(verb)* costare
  what does it cost? quanto costa?
cotton il cotone
cotton wool il cotone idrofilo
cough *(noun)* la tosse
  (verb) tossire
country *(state)* il paese
  (not town) la campagna
cousin il cugino
  (female) la cugina
crab il granchio
cramp il crampo
crayfish il gambero
cream *(for cake etc)* la crema, la
  panna
  (lotion) la crema
credit card la carta di credito
crew l'equipaggio
crisps le patatine
crowded affollato
cruise la crociera
crutches le stampelle
cry *(verb: weep)* piangere
  (shout) gridare
cucumber il cetriolo
cufflinks i gemelli
cup la tazza
cupboard l'armadio
curlers i bigodini
curls i ricci
curry il curry
curtain la tenda
customs la dogana
cut *(noun)* il taglio
  (verb) tagliare

dad il papà, il babbo
damp umido
dance *(noun)* il ballo
  (verb) ballare

dangerous pericoloso
dark scuro
daughter la figlia
day il giorno
dead morto
deaf sordo
dear caro
deckchair la sedia a sdraio
deep profondo
delayed in ritardo
deliberately deliberatamente
dentist il/la dentista
dentures la dentiera
deodorant il deodorante
department store il grande
  magazzino
departure la partenza
departure lounge la sala d'attesa
develop *(film)* sviluppare
diamond *(jewel)* il diamante
diamonds *(cards)* quadri
diary il diario
dictionary il dizionario
die morire
diesel il diesel
different diverso
  that's different! è diverso!
  I'd like a different one ne vorrei
  un altro
difficult difficile
dining room la sala da pranzo
dinner la cena
directory *(telephone)* la guida
  telefonica
dirty sporco
disabled invalido
disposable nappies i pannolini usa e
  getta
distributor *(in car)* il distributore
dive *(noun)* il tuffo
  (verb) tuffarsi
diving board il trampolino
divorced divorziato
do fare

how do you do? piacere di conoscerla

doctor il dottore
(female) la dottoressa

document il documento

dog il cane

doll la bambola

dollar il dollaro

door la porta

double room la camera doppia

doughnut il krapfen

down giù

drawing pin la puntina da disegno

dress il vestito

drink *(noun)* la bibita
(verb) bere
would you like a drink? vorresti qualcosa da bere?

drinking water l'acqua potabile

drive *(verb)* guidare

driver il guidatore
(female) la guidatrice
(of bus, lorry etc) l'autista

driving licence la patente di guida

drunk ubriaco

dry asciutto
(wine) secco

dry-cleaner's la lavanderia a secco

dummy *(for baby)* la tettarella

during durante

dustbin la pattumiera

duster lo straccio per la polvere

duty-free il duty free

duvet il piumino

each *(every)* ogni
a thousand lire each mille lire ciascuno

ear l'orecchio
ears le orecchie

early presto

earrings gli orecchini

east l'est

easy facile

eat mangiare

EC la CEE

egg l'uovo

either: either them l'uno o l'altro
either ... or ... o... o...

elastic elastico

elastic band l'elastico

elbow il gomito

electric elettrico

electricity l'elettricità

else: something else qualcos'altro
someone else qualcun'altro
somewhere else da qualche altra parte

embarrassing imbarazzante

embassy l'ambasciata

embroidery il ricamo

emergency l'emergenza

emergency brake il freno d'emergenza

emergency exit l'uscita di sicurezza

empty vuoto

end la fine

engaged *(couple)* fidanzato
(occupied) occupato

engine *(motor)* il motore
(railway) la locomotiva

England l'Inghilterra

English inglese

Englishman l'inglese

Englishwoman l'inglese

enlargement l'ampliamento

enough abbastanza

entrance l'entrata

envelope la busta

escalator la scala mobile

especially particolarmente

estate agent l'agente immobiliare

evening la sera

every ogni

everyone ognuno, tutti

everything tutto

everywhere dappertutto

example l'esempio

for example per esempio
excellent ottimo, eccellente
excess baggage il bagaglio in eccesso
exchange (verb) scambiare
exchange rate il tasso di cambio
excursion l'escursione
excuse me! (to get past) permesso!
(to get attention) mi scusi!
(when sneezing etc) scusate!
exit l'uscita
expensive caro, costoso
extension lead la prolunga
eye l'occhio
eyes gli occhi

face la faccia
faint (unclear) indistinto
(verb) svenire
fair (funfair) il luna park
(trade) la fiera
it's not fair non è giusto
false teeth la dentiera
family la famiglia
fan (ventilator) il ventilatore
(enthusiast) l'ammiratore
fan belt la cinghia della ventola
fantastic fantastico
far lontano
how far is it to …? quanto dista da qui…?
fare la tariffa
farm la fattoria
farmer l'agricoltore
fashion la moda
fast veloce
fat (person) grasso
(on meat etc) il grasso
father il padre
fax (noun) il fax
(verb: document) spedire via fax
feel (touch) tastare
I feel hot ho caldo
I feel like … ho voglia di…

I don't feel well non mi sento bene
felt-tip pen il pennarello
fence lo steccato
ferry il traghetto
fever la febbre
fiancé il fidanzato
fiancée la fidanzata
field il campo
filling (in tooth) l'otturazione
(in sandwich, cake etc) il ripieno
film (for camera) la pellicola
(at cinema) il film
filter il filtro
finger il dito
fire il fuoco
(blaze) l'incendio
fire extinguisher l'estintore
fireworks i fuochi d'artificio
first primo
first aid il pronto soccorso
first floor il primo piano
fish il pesce
fishing la pesca
to go fishing andare a pesca
fishmonger's il pescivendolo
fizzy frizzante
flag la bandiera
flash (camera) il flash
flat (apartment) l'appartamento
(level) piatto
flavour il gusto
flea la pulce
flight il volo
flip-flops gli infradito
flippers le pinne
floor (storey) il piano
(ground) il pavimento
flour la farina
Florence Firenze
flower il fiore
flute il flauto
fly (insect) la mosca
(verb) volare

I'm flying to London sto andando a Londra in aereo
fog la nebbia
folk music la musica folk
food il cibo
food poisoning l'intossicazione alimentare
foot il piede
football *(game)* il calcio
(ball) il pallone
for per
for me per me
what for? per che cosa?
foreigner lo straniero
forest la foresta
forget dimenticare
fork *(for food)* la forchetta
fortnight due settimane
fountain pen la penna stilografica
fourth quarto
France la Francia
free *(not engaged)* libero
(no charge) gratis
freezer il congelatore
French francese
Frenchman il francese
Frenchwoman la francese
fridge il frigorifero
friend l'amico
(female) l'amica
friendly cordiale
fringe *(hair)* la frangia
front: in front of you davanti a te
frost il gelo
fruit la frutta
fruit juice il succo di frutta
fry friggere
frying pan la padella
full pieno
I'm full (up) sono sazio
full board la pensione completa
funny divertente
(odd) strano
furniture i mobili

garage il garage
garden il giardino
garlic l'aglio
gas-permeable lenses le lenti semi-rigide
gate il cancello
(at airport) l'uscita
gay *(homosexual)* omosessuale, gay
gear *(car)* il cambio
gear lever la leva del cambio
gel *(hair)* il gel
Genoa Genova
gents *(toilet)* la toilette degli uomini
German *(man)* il tedesco
(woman) la tedesca
(adj) tedesco
Germany la Germania
get *(obtain)* ricevere
(fetch: person) chiamare
(something) prendere
have you got ...? ha...?
to get the train prendere il treno
get back: we get back tomorrow torniamo domani
to get something back riavere indietro qualcosa
get in entrare
(arrive) arrivare
get off *(bus etc)* scendere (da)
get on *(bus etc)* salire (su)
get out uscire (da)
get up alzarsi
gift il regalo
gin il gin
ginger *(spice)* lo zenzero
girl la ragazza
girlfriend la ragazza
give dare
glad contento
glass *(material)* il vetro
(for drinking) il bicchiere
glasses gli occhiali
gloss prints le fotografie su carta lucida

gloves i guanti
glue la colla
go andare
  (depart) partire
gold l'oro
good buono
  good! bene!
goodbye arrivederci
government il governo
granddaughter la nipote
grandfather il nonno
grandmother la nonna
grandparents i nonni
grandson il nipote
grapes l'uva
grass l'erba
Great Britain la Gran Bretagna
Greece la Grecia
Greek *(man)* il greco
  (woman) la greca
  (adj) greco
green verde
grey grigio
grill la griglia
grocer's il negozio di alimentari
ground floor il pianterreno
groundsheet il telone
  impermeabile
guarantee *(noun)* la garanzia
  (verb) garantire
guard la guardia
guide *(person)* la guida
guide book la guida
guitar la chitarra
gun *(rifle)* il fucile
  (pistol) la pistola

hair i capelli
haircut il taglio
hairdresser's il parrucchiere
hair dryer l'asciugacapelli
hair spray la lacca per i capelli
half metà
  half an hour mezz'ora

half board mezza pensione
ham il prosciutto
hamburger l'hamburger
hammer il martello
hand la mano
handbag la borsetta
handbrake il freno a mano
handkerchief il fazzoletto
handle *(door)* la maniglia
handsome bello, attraente
hangover i postumi della sbornia
happy felice
harbour il porto
hard duro
  (difficult) difficile
hard lenses le lenti rigide
hardware shop il negozio di
  ferramenta
hat il cappello
have avere
  I don't have ... non ho...
  have you got ...? ha...?
  I have to go now devo andare
  adesso
he lui
head la testa
headache il mal di testa
headlights i fari
hear udire, sentire
hearing aid l'apparecchio acustico
heart il cuore
hearts *(cards)* cuori
heater il termosifone
heating il riscaldamento
heavy pesante
heel *(of foot)* il tallone
  (of shoe) il tacco
hello ciao
  (on phone) pronto
help *(noun)* l'aiuto
  (verb) aiutare
her: it's her è lei
  it's for her è per lei
  give it to her daglielo

her book il suo libro
her house la sua casa
her shoes le sue scarpe
her dresses i suoi vestiti
it's hers è suo
hi! salve!
high alto
highway code il codice della strada
hill la collina
him: it's him è lui
it's for him è per lui
give it to him daglielo
hire *(car, bike)* noleggiare
his: his book il suo libro
his house la sua casa
his shoes le sue scarpe
his socks i suoi calzini
it's his è suo
history la storia
hitchhike fare l'autostop
hobby il passatempo
holiday la vacanza
home: at home a casa
honest onesto
honey il miele
honeymoon la luna di miele
horn *(car)* il clacson
(animal) il corno
horrible orribile
hospital l'ospedale
hour l'ora
house la casa
how? come?
hungry: I'm hungry ho fame
hurry: I'm in a hurry ho fretta
husband il marito

I io
ice il ghiaccio
ice cream il gelato
ice lolly il ghiacciolo
ice skates i pattini da ghiaccio
if se
ignition l'accensione

ill malato
immediately immediatamente
impossible impossibile
in: in English in inglese
in the hotel nell'albergo
in Venice a Venezia
indicator l'indicatore di direzione
indigestion l'indigestione
infection l'infezione
information le informazioni
injection l'iniezione
injury la ferita
ink l'inchiostro
inner tube la camera d'aria
insect l'insetto
insect repellent l'insettifugo
insomnia l'insonnia
instant coffee il caffè solubile
insurance l'assicurazione
interesting interessante
interpret interpretare
interpreter l'interprete
invitation l'invito
Ireland l'Irlanda
Irish irlandese
Irishman l'irlandese
Irishwoman l'irlandese
iron *(material)* il ferro
(for clothes) il ferro da stiro
(verb) stirare
is: he/she/it is ... (lui/lei/esso) è...
island l'isola
it esso
Italian *(man)* l'italiano
(woman) l'italiana
(adj) italiano
the Italians gli italiani
Italy Italia
its suo

jacket la giacca
jam la marmellata
jazz il jazz
jeans i jeans

jellyfish la medusa
jeweller il gioielliere
job il lavoro
jog *(verb)* fare jogging
  to go for a jog andare a fare jogging
jogging il jogging
joke lo scherzo
journey il viaggio
jumper il maglione
just *(only)* solo
  it's just arrived è appena arrivato

kettle il bollitore
key la chiave
kidney il rene
kilo il chilo
kilometre il chilometro
kitchen la cucina
knee il ginocchio
knife il coltello
knit lavorare a maglia
knitwear la maglieria
know sapere
  (person) conoscere
  I don't know non so

label l'etichetta
lace il pizzo
laces *(of shoe)* i lacci
ladies *(toilet)* la toilette delle donne
lady la signora
lake il lago
lamb l'agnello
lamp la lampada
lampshade il paralume
land *(noun)* la terra
  (verb) atterrare
language la lingua
large grande
last *(final)* ultimo
  last week la settimana scorsa
  at last! finalmente!

late: it's getting late si sta facendo tardi
  the bus is late l'autobus è in ritardo
later più tardi
laugh ridere
laundry *(place)* la lavanderia
  (dirty clothes) la biancheria
laxative il lassativo
lazy pigro
leaf la foglia
leaflet il volantino
learn imparare
leather la pelle, il cuoio
left *(not right)* sinistra
  there's nothing left non c'è rimasto più nulla
left-luggage locker il desposito bagagli
leg la gamba
lemon il limone
lemonade la limonata
length la lunghezza
lens la lente
less meno
lesson la lezione
letter la lettera
letter box la cassetta delle lettere
lettuce la lattuga
library la biblioteca
licence la patente
life la vita
lift *(in building)* l'ascensore
  could you give me a lift? può darmi un passaggio?
light *(noun)* la luce
  (adj: not heavy) leggero
  (not dark) chiaro
light bulb la lampadina
light meter l'esposimetro
lighter l'accendino
lighter fuel il gas per accendini
like: I like you mi piaci
  I like swimming mi piace nuotare

it's like ... assomiglia a...
  like this one come questo
lime *(fruit)* il lime
lip salve il burro di cacao
lipstick il rossetto
liqueur il liquore
list l'elenco
litre il litro
litter i rifiuti
little *(small)* piccolo
  it's a little big è un po' grande
  just a little solo un po'
liver il fegato
lobster l'aragosta
lollipop il lecca lecca
long lungo
  how long does it take? quanto ci vuole?
long-distance *(call)* interurbano
lorry il camion
lost property office l'ufficio oggetti smarriti
lot: a lot molto
loud forte
  (colour) chiassoso
love *(verb)* amare
lover l'amante
low basso
luck la fortuna
  good luck! buona fortuna!
luggage i bagagli
luggage rack la reticella (per i bagagli)
lunch il pranzo

mad pazzo
magazine la rivista
mail la posta
make fare
make-up il trucco
man l'uomo
manager il direttore
manageress la direttrice
many: not many non molti

map la carta (geografica)
  a map of Rome una piantina di Roma
marble il marmo
margarine la margarina
market il mercato
marmalade la marmellata d'arance
married sposato
mascara il mascara
mass *(church)* la messa
mast l'albero
match *(light)* il fiammifero
  (sport) l'incontro
material *(cloth)* la stoffa
matter: it doesn't matter non importa
mattress il materasso
maybe forse
me: it's me sono io
  it's for me è per me
  give it to me dammelo
meal il pasto
mean: what does this mean? che cosa significa?
meat la carne
mechanic il meccanico
medicine la medicina
Mediterranean il Mediterraneo
meeting l'incontro
melon il melone
menu il menù
message il messaggio
midday mezzogiorno
middle: in the middle of the square in mezzo alla piazza
  in the middle of the night nel cuore della notte
midnight mezzanotte
Milan Milano
milk il latte
mine: it's mine è mio
mineral water l'acqua minerale
minute il minuto
mirror lo specchio

Miss Signorina
mistake l'errore
money i soldi
month il mese
monument il monumento
moon la luna
moped il motorino
more: more than ... più di...
  I want some more ne voglio
  ancora
morning la mattina
  in the morning di mattina
mosaic il mosaico
mosquito la zanzara
mother la madre
motorbike la motocicletta
motorboat il motoscafo
motorway l'autostrada
mountain la montagna
mountain bike la mountain bike
mouse il topo
mousse *(for hair)* la schiuma
moustache i baffi
mouth la bocca
move *(verb)* muovere
  (move house) traslocare
  don't move! non muoverti!
Mr Signor
Mrs Signora
much: much better molto meglio
  much slower molto più
  lentamente
  not much non molto
mug il tazzone
mum mamma
museum il museo
mushroom il fungo
music la musica
musical instrument lo strumento
  musicale
musician il musicista
mussels le cozze
must: I must devo
mustard la senape

my: my book il mio libro
  my bag la mia borsa
  my keys le mie chiavi
  my dresses i miei vestiti

nail *(metal)* il chiodo
  (finger) l'unghia
nail clippers il tagliaunghie
nail file la limetta per le unghie
nail polish lo smalto per le unghie
name il nome
  what's your name? come ti
  chiami?
Naples Napoli
nappy il pannolino
narrow stretto
near: near the door vicino alla
  porta
necessary necessario
neck il collo
necklace la collana
need: I need ... ho bisogno di...
  there's no need non c'è bisogno
needle l'ago
negative *(photo)* la negativa
neither: neither of them nè l'uno
  nè l'altro
  neither ... nor ... nè... nè...
nephew il nipote
never mai
  I never smoke non fumo mai
new nuovo
news le notizie
  (on radio) il notiziario
newsagent il giornalaio
newspaper il giornale
New Zealand la Nuova Zelanda
New Zealander *(man)* il
  neozelandese
  (woman) la neozelandese
  (adj) neozelandese
next prossimo
  next week la settimana prossima
  what next? e poi?

who's next? a chi tocca?
nice *(attractive)* carino, bello
(pleasant) simpatico
(to eat) buono
niece la nipote
night la notte
nightclub il night
nightdress la camicia da notte
night porter il portiere di notte
no *(response)* no
I have no money non ho soldi
nobody nessuno
noisy rumoroso
north il nord
Northern Ireland l'Irlanda del
Nord
nose il naso
not non
he's not ... non è...
notebook il taccuino
nothing niente
novel il romanzo
now ora, adesso
nowhere da nessuna parte
nudist il/la nudista
number il numero
number plate la targa
nursery slope la discesa per
principianti
nut la noce, la nocciola
(for bolt) il dado

oars i remi
occasionally ogni tanto
octopus la piovra
of di
office l'ufficio
often spesso
oil l'olio
ointment l'unguento
OK OK
old vecchio
how old are you? quanti anni
hai?

olive l'oliva
olive oil l'olio d'oliva
omelette l'omelette
on su
on the table sul tavolo
a book on Venice un libro su
Venezia
on Monday di lunedì
one uno
onion la cipolla
only solo
open *(adj)* aperto
(verb) aprire
operation l'operazione
operator l'operatore
(female) l'operatrice
opposite: opposite the hotel di
fronte all'albergo
optician l'ottico
or o
orange *(fruit)* l'arancia
(colour) arancione
orange juice il succo d'arancia
orchestra l'orchestra
ordinary normale
organ *(music)* l'organo
other: the other (one) l'altro
our: our hotel il nostro albergo
our car la nostra macchina
it's ours è nostro
out: he's out è uscito
outside fuori
oven il forno
over *(above)* su, sopra
over 100 più di cento
over the river al di là del fiume
it's over *(finished)* è finito
over there laggiù
overtake sorpassare
oyster l'ostrica

pack of cards il mazzo di carte
package *(parcel)* il pacco
packet il pacchetto

padlock il lucchetto
Padua Padova
page la pagina
pain il dolore
paint la vernice
pair il paio
palace il palazzo
pale pallido
pancakes le frittelle
paper la carta
   (newspaper) il giornale
paracetamol la cibalgina ®
paraffin la paraffina
parcel il pacchetto
pardon? prego?
parents i genitori
park *(noun)* il parco
   (verb) parcheggiare
parsley il prezzemolo
parting *(hair)* la riga
party *(celebration)* la festa
   (group) il gruppo
   (political) il partito
passenger il passeggero
   (female) la passeggera
passport il passaporto
pasta la pasta
path il sentiero
pavement il marciapiede
pay pagare
peach la pesca
peanuts le arachidi
pear la pera
pearl la perla
peas i piselli
pedestrian il pedone
peg *(clothes)* la molletta
   (tent) il picchetto
pen la penna
pencil la matita
pencil sharpener il temperamatite
penfriend il/la corrispondente
penknife il temperino
people la gente

pepper il pepe
   (red, green) il peperone
peppermint la menta piperita
per: per person a persona
   per annum all'anno
perfect perfetto
perfume il profumo
perhaps forse
perm la permanente
petrol la benzina
petrol station la stazione di servizio
photograph *(noun)* la fotografia
   (verb) fotografare
photographer il fotografo
phrase book il vocabolarietto
piano il pianoforte
pickpocket il borsaiolo
picnic il picnic
piece il pezzo
pillow il cuscino
pin lo spillo
pineapple l'ananas
pink rosa
pipe *(for smoking)* la pipa
   (for water) il tubo
piston il pistone
pizza la pizza
place il posto
   at your place a casa tua
plant la pianta
plaster *(for cut)* il cerotto
plastic la plastica
plastic bag il sacchetto di plastica
plate il piatto
platform il binario
play *(theatre)* la commedia
   (verb) giocare
please per favore
plug *(electrical)* la spina
   (sink) il tappo
pocket la tasca
poison il veleno
police la polizia
policeman il poliziotto

police station la stazione di polizia
politics la politica
poor povero
  poor quality di cattiva qualità
Pope il Papa
pop music la musica pop
pork la carne di maiale
port il porto
porter *(hotel)* il portiere
possible possibile
post *(noun)* la posta
  (verb) spedire per posta
post box la buca delle lettere
postcard la cartolina
poster il manifesto
postman il postino
post office l'ufficio postale
potato la patata
poultry il pollame
pound *(money)* la sterlina
  (weight) la libbra
powder *(cosmetic)* la cipria
pram la carrozzina
prawn il gambero
  (bigger) il gamberone
prefer preferire
prescription la ricetta
pretty *(beautiful)* grazioso, carino
  (quite) piuttosto
priest il prete
private privato
problem il problema
protection factor il fattore di
  protezione
public pubblico
pull tirare
puncture la foratura
purple viola
purse il borsellino
push spingere
pushchair il passeggino
put mettere
pyjamas il pigiama

quality la qualità
quarter il quarto
quay il molo
question la domanda
queue *(noun)* la fila
  (verb) fare la fila
quick veloce
quiet tranquillo
quite *(fairly)* abbastanza
  (fully) molto

radiator il radiatore
radio la radio
radish il ravanello
railway la ferrovia
rain la pioggia
raincoat l'impermeabile
raisins l'uvetta
rare *(uncommon)* raro
  (steak) al sangue
raspberry il lampone
rat il ratto
razor blades le lamette
read leggere
reading lamp la lampada da studio
ready pronto
rear lights i fari posteriori
receipt *(restaurants, hotels)* la ricevuta
  (shops, bars) lo scontrino
receptionist il/la receptionist
record *(music)* il disco
  (sporting etc) il record
record player il giradischi
record shop il negozio di dischi
red rosso
refreshments i rinfreschi
relax rilassarsi
religion la religione
remember ricordare
  I don't remember non ricordo
rent *(verb: flat)* affittare
reservation la prenotazione
rest *(noun: remainder)* il resto
  (verb: relax) riposarsi

restaurant il ristorante
restaurant car il vagone ristorante
return ritornare
(give back) restituire
return ticket il biglietto di andata e
ritorno
rice il riso
rich ricco
right *(correct)* giusto, esatto
(not left) destro
ring *(noun: wedding etc)* l'anello
(verb: phone) telefonare
ripe maturo
river il fiume
road la strada
rock *(stone)* la roccia
(music) il rock
roll *(bread)* il panino
Roman Forum il Foro Romano
Rome Roma
roof il tetto
room la stanza
(space) lo spazio
rope la corda
rose la rosa
round *(circular)* rotondo
it's my round tocca a me
offrire
row remare
rowing boat la barca a remi
rubber la gomma
rubbish le immondizie
ruby *(stone)* il rubino
rucksack lo zaino
rug *(mat)* il tappeto
(blanket) il plaid
ruins le rovine, i resti
ruler *(for drawing)* la riga
rum il rum
run *(verb)* correre

sad triste
safe *(not dangerous)* sicuro
safety pin la spilla di sicurezza

St Mark's Square Piazza San
Marco
St Peter's San Pietro
salad l'insalata
salami il salame
sale *(at reduced prices)* i saldi
salmon il salmone
salt il sale
same: the same dress lo stesso
vestito
same again please un altro, per
favore
sand la sabbia
sandals i sandali
sand dunes le dune
sandwich il panino
sanitary towels gli assorbenti
(igienici)
Sardinia la Sardegna
sauce la salsa
saucepan la pentola
sauna la sauna
sausage la salsiccia
say dire
what did you say? che cosa ha
detto?
how do you say ...? come si
dice...?
scarf la sciarpa
(head) il foulard
school la scuola
scissors le forbici
Scotland la Scozia
Scotsman lo scozzese
Scotswoman la scozzese
Scottish scozzese
screw la vite
screwdriver il cacciavite
sea il mare
seafood i frutti di mare
seat il posto
seat belt la cintura di sicurezza
second secondo
see vedere

I can't see non vedo
I see capisco
sell vendere
sellotape ® lo scotch ®
separate *(adj)* separato
separated *(couple)* separati
serious serio
serviette il tovagliolo
several diversi
sew cucire
shampoo lo shampoo
shave: to have a shave radersi
shaving foam la schiuma da barba
shawl lo scialle
she lei
sheet il lenzuolo
shell la conchiglia
shellfish *(crabs etc)* i crostacei
(molluscs) i molluschi
sherry lo sherry
ship la nave
shirt la camicia
shoe laces i lacci per le scarpe
shoe polish il lucido per le scarpe
shoes le scarpe
shop il negozio
shopping la spesa
to go shopping andare a fare
acquisti
(for food) andare a fare la spesa
short corto
shorts gli shorts
shoulder la spalla
shower la doccia
(rain) l'acquazzone
shrimp il gamberetto
shutter *(camera)* l'otturatore
(window) l'imposta
Sicily la Sicilia
side *(edge)* il lato
sidelights le luci di posizione
sights: the sights of ... le
attrazioni turistiche di...
silk la seta

silver *(colour)* d'argento
(metal) l'argento
simple semplice
sing cantare
single *(one)* solo
(unmarried: man) celibe
(woman) nubile
single room la camera singola
single ticket la biglietto di sola
andata
sister la sorella
skid slittare
skiing: to go skiing andare a sciare
skin cleanser il latte detergente
ski resort la località sciistica
skirt la gonna
skis gli sci
sky il cielo
sleep *(noun)* il sonno
(verb) dormire
sleeper *(on train)* il vagone letto
sleeping bag il sacco a pelo
sleeping pill il sonnifero
slippers le pantofole
slow lento
small piccolo
smell *(noun)* l'odore
(verb: stink) puzzare
smile *(noun)* il sorriso
(verb) sorridere
smoke *(noun)* il fumo
(verb) fumare
snack lo spuntino
snorkel il respiratore a tubo
snow la neve
so: so good così bene
not so much non così tanto
soaking solution *(for contact lenses)* il
liquido per lenti
soap il sapone
socks i calzini
soda water l'acqua di seltz
soft lenses le lenti morbide
somebody qualcuno

somehow in qualche modo
something qualcosa
sometimes qualche volta
somewhere da qualche parte
son il figlio
song la canzone
sorry! scusi!
  I'm sorry mi dispiace
  sorry? *(pardon)* come?, scusi?
soup la zuppa
south il sud
souvenir il souvenir
spade *(shovel)* la vanga
spades *(cards)* picche
Spain la Spagna
Spanish spagnolo
spanner la chiave fissa
spares i pezzi di ricambio
spark plug la candela
speak parlare
  do you speak ...? parla...?
  I don't speak ... non parlo...
speed la velocità
spider il ragno
spinach gli spinaci
spoon il cucchiaio
spring *(mechanical)* la molla
  (season) la primavera
square *(noun: in town)* la piazza
  (adj: shape) quadrato
staircase la scala
stairs le scale
stamp il francobollo
stapler la cucitrice
star la stella
  (film) la star
start *(noun)* l'inizio
  (verb) cominciare
station la stazione
statue la statua
steak la bistecca
steal rubare
  it's been stolen è stato rubato
steamer *(boat)* la nave a vapore

  (for cooking) la pentola a pressione
stockings le calze
stomach lo stomaco
stomach ache il mal di stomaco
stop *(noun: bus)* la fermata
  dell'autobus
  (verb) fermare
  stop! alt!, fermo!
storm la tempesta
strawberry la fragola
stream il ruscello
street la strada
string *(cord)* lo spago
  (guitar etc) la corda
strong forte
student lo studente
  (female) la studentessa
stupid stupido
suburbs la periferia
sugar lo zucchero
suit *(noun)* il completo
  it suits you ti sta bene
suitcase la valigia
sun il sole
sunbathe prendere il sole
sunburn la scottatura
sunglasses gli occhiali da sole
sunny: it's sunny c'è il sole
sunshade l'ombrellone
suntan: to get a suntan abbronzarsi
suntan lotion la lozione solare
suntanned abbronzato
supermarket il supermercato
supper la cena
supplement il supplemento
sure sicuro
  are you sure? sei sicuro?
surname il cognome
sweat *(noun)* il sudore
  (verb) sudare
sweatshirt la felpa
sweet *(not sour)* dolce
  (candy) la caramella
swim *(verb)* nuotare

swimming costume il costume da bagno
swimming pool la piscina
swimming trunks il costume da bagno (per uomo)
Swiss *(man)* lo svizzero
    (woman) la svizzera
    (adj) svizzero
switch l'interruttore
Switzerland la Svizzera
synagogue la sinagoga

table il tavolo
tablet la compressa
take prendere
take away: to take away da portare via
take-off il decollo
talcum powder il talco
talk *(noun)* la conversazione
    (verb) parlare
tall alto
tampons i tamponi
tangerine il mandarino
tap il rubinetto
tapestry l'arazzo
tea il tè
teacher l'insegnante
tea towel lo strofinaccio
telegram il telegramma
telephone *(noun)* il telefono
    (verb) telefonare
telephone box la cabina telefonica
telephone call la telefonata
television la televisione
temperature la temperatura
    (fever) la febbre
tent la tenda
tent pole il palo della tenda
than di
thank *(verb)* ringraziare
    thank you/thanks grazie
that: that one quello
    that country quel paese

that man quell'uomo
that woman quella donna
what's that? cos'è quello?
I think that ... penso che...
the *(see page 5)*
their: their room la loro stanza
    their friend il loro amico
    their books i loro libri
    their pens le loro penne
    it's theirs è loro
them: it's them sono loro
    it's for them è per loro
    give it to them dallo a loro
then poi, allora
there là
    there is/are ... c'è/ci sono...
    is/are there ...? c'è/ci sono...?
Thermos flask ® il thermos
these: these things queste cose
    these boys questi ragazzi
they loro
thick spesso
thin sottile
think pensare
    I think so penso di sì
    I'll think about it ci penserò
third terzo
thirsty: I'm thirsty ho sete
this: this one questo
    this picture questo quadro
    this man quest'uomo
    this woman questa donna
    what's this? cos'è questo?
    this is Mr ... (questo è) il signor...
those: those things quelle cose
    those boys quei ragazzi
throat la gola
throat pastilles le pasticche per la gola
through attraverso
thunderstorm il temporale
Tiber il Tevere
ticket il biglietto
ticket office la biglietteria

tide la marea
tie *(noun)* la cravatta
  (verb) legare
tight *(clothes)* stretto
tights i collant
time il tempo
  what's the time? che ore sono?
timetable l'orario
tin la scatola
tin-opener l'apriscatole
tip *(money)* la mancia
  (end) la punta
tired stanco
tissues i fazzolettini di carta
to: to England in Inghilterra
  to the station alla stazione
  to the doctor dal dottore
  to the centre in centro
toast il pane tostato
tobacco il tabacco
today oggi
together insieme
toilet la toilette
toilet paper la carta igienica
tomato il pomodoro
tomato juice il succo di pomodoro
tomorrow domani
tongue la lingua
tonic l'acqua tonica
tonight stasera
too *(also)* anche
  (excessively) troppo
tooth il dente
toothache il mal di denti
toothbrush lo spazzolino da denti
toothpaste il dentifricio
torch la torcia elettrica
tour il giro
tourist il/la turista
tourist office l'ufficio turistico
towel l'asciugamano
tower la torre
  the Leaning Tower of Pisa la
  Torre di Pisa

town la città
town hall il municipio
toy il giocattolo
toy shop il negozio di giocattoli
tracksuit la tuta da ginnastica
tractor il trattore
tradition la tradizione
traffic il traffico
traffic jam l'ingorgo
traffic lights il semaforo
trailer il rimorchio
train il treno
trainers le scarpe da ginnastica
translate tradurre
translator il traduttore
  (female) la traduttrice
travel agency l'agenzia di viaggio
traveller's cheque il traveller's
  cheque
tray il vassoio
tree l'albero
trousers i pantaloni
true vero
try provare
Turin Torino
tunnel il tunnel
Tuscany la Toscana
tweezers le pinzette
typewriter la macchina da scrivere
tyre la gomma

umbrella l'ombrello
uncle lo zio
under ... sotto...
underground la metropolitana
underpants le mutande
underskirt la sottoveste
understand capire
  I don't understand non capisco
underwear la biancheria intima
university l'università
unleaded senza piombo
until fino a
unusual insolito

up su
  (upwards) verso l'alto
  up there lassù
urgent urgente
us: it's us siamo noi
  it's for us è per noi
  give it to us daccelo
use *(noun)* l'uso
  (verb) usare
  it's no use non serve a niente
useful utile
usual solito
usually di solito

vacancy *(room)* la stanza libera
vacuum flask il thermos
valley la valle
valve la valvola
vanilla la vaniglia
vase il vaso
Vatican City la Città del Vaticano
veal la carne di vitello
vegetables la verdura
vegetarian vegetariano
vehicle il veicolo
Venice Venezia
very molto
  very much moltissimo
vest la canottiera
video *(tape/film)* il video
video recorder il videoregistratore
view la vista
viewfinder il mirino
villa la villa
village il villaggio
vinegar l'aceto
violin il violino
visit *(noun)* la visita
  (verb) andare a trovare
visitor l'ospite
vitamin tablet la compressa di vitamine
vodka la vodka
voice la voce

wait aspettare
  wait! aspetta!
waiter il cameriere
  waiter! cameriere!
waiting room la sala d'attesa
waitress la cameriera
  waitress! cameriera!
Wales il Galles
walk *(noun: stroll)* la passeggiata
  (verb) camminare
  to go for a walk andare a fare una passeggiata
walkman ® il walkman ®
wall il muro
wallet il portafoglio
war la guerra
wardrobe il guardaroba
warm caldo
was: I was (io) ero
  he/she/it was (lui/lei/esso) era
washer *(for tap)* la rondella
washing powder il detersivo (per bucato)
washing-up liquid il detersivo liquido per piatti
wasp la vespa
watch *(noun)* l'orologio
  (verb) guardare
water l'acqua
waterfall la cascata
water heater lo scaldaacqua
wave *(noun)* l'onda
  (verb: with hand) salutare
wavy: wavy hair i capelli ondulati
we noi
weather il tempo
wedding il matrimonio
week la settimana
welcome benvenuto
  you're welcome di niente, prego
wellingtons gli stivali di gomma
Welsh gallese
Welshman il gallese
Welshwoman la gallese**

were: you were (Lei) era
  (singular, familiar) (tu) eri
  (plural) (voi) eravate
  we were (noi) eravamo
  they were (loro) erano
west l'ovest
wet bagnato
what? cosa?
wheel la ruota
wheelchair la sedia a rotelle
when? quando?
where? dove?
whether se
which? quale?
whisky il whisky
white bianco
who? chi?
why? perchè?
wide ampio
wife la moglie
wind il vento
window la finestra
windscreen il parabrezza
wine il vino
wing l'ala
with con
without senza
woman la donna
wood *(material)* il legno
wool la lana
word la parola
work *(noun)* il lavoro
  (verb) lavorare

(machine) funzionare
worse peggiore
worst il peggiore
wrapping paper la carta da
  imballaggio
  (for presents) la carta da regalo
wrist il polso
writing paper la carta da scrivere
wrong sbagliato

year l'anno
yellow giallo
yes sì
yesterday ieri
yet ancora
  not yet non ancora
yoghurt lo yogurt
you Lei
  (singular, familiar) tu
  (plural) voi
your: your book il suo libro
  your shirt la sua camicia
  your trousers le sue scarpe
  (singular, familiar)
  your book il tuo libro
  your shirt la tua camicia
  your shoes le tue scarpe
yours: is this yours? è suo?
  (singular, familiar) è tuo?
youth hostel l'ostello della gioventù

zip la chiusura lampo
zoo lo zoo